WHAT OUR READERS ARE SAYING

Regardless of where you are on your personal journey toward enlightenment and self-mastery, *PEACE: Power Up Your Life* is a personal transformation life changer!

Mary Giuseffi, Author, *Straight Up With A Twist*

Simply put, the Biskinds have done it again with the second book in their *CODEBREAKER PLATINUM Series.* By any measure, this book is destined to make contributions unmatched in such areas as love's importance, power, jump-starting the process, rating your state of love, and how to become the best version of yourself. Enlightenment seems to fly off every page into our minds and hearts.

William Bryant – Former Chairman of the Board, American Chamber of Commerce Executives

Sandra and Daniel Biskind ....extraordinary spiritual/personal growth leaders have nailed the formula that allows us to remove all the stressors that stand in the way of great peacefulness and resourcefulness.

Jackie Lapin, Author - *Practical Conscious Creation*

Over the years I have attended dozens of Sandra and Daniel's workshops. To say their tools have impacted my life in a dramatic way is an understatement. Their new book *Peace: Power Up Your Life* is chock full with strategies that can dissolve self- defeating mind programs and lead one to a life of peace and joy.

Alexi Neocleous, CEO and Chief Strategist, Marketing Bump

Your book, *PEACE: Power Up Your Life,* made my jaw drop...the most incredible gift God has ever given me. And He worked through you to show me.

Molly Cochran

Everyone who thinks that living the life they dream about is out of reach, or out of their hands should read this amazing book. I want to give this book to all the people I love so they can experience more Peace, too!

Esther Anderson, Gold Logie-nominated actor, host and international model

PEACE: Power Up Your Life has opened up my world to living a stress free, happy, and healthy life! The book has clear and easy to use tools... Wonderful read, everyone should have this knowledge as they embark on their life journeys.

Benjamin Seiden

Sandra and Daniel Biskind are "the Real Deal".....just buy this book and start a wondrous journey that will deliver for you exactly what they promise....PEACE!!!

Robert Hurst, Owner, Alchemy Consulting

ACCLAIM FOR SANDRA AND DANIEL BISKIND

JACK CANFIELD – Co-author of *Chicken Soup for the Soul* series, *The Success Principles,* and a featured teacher in the film *The Secret*

Sandra and Daniel are profound healers, trainers, speakers, and authors who do some exceptional transformational work. I've experienced their work and found it truly life changing — so much so that I had them work with my entire staff, with magical results. They have an amazing ability to shift energy and remove blocks on very deep levels.

From the first time I sat down with them, I knew something special and profound was about to happen. Their unconditional love, joy, and radiance fill the room. An hour later, I left more calm, more centered, more my true self, and more creative than I can remember. They are the real deal, and I highly recommend them and their work. It is transformational wizardry at its best.

DEREK RYDAL – Transformational coach, best-selling author, creator of *The Law of Emergence*

I've worked with a lot of healers, but rarely do I meet one who is as quick to the heart of the matter as Sandra. In a matter of minutes, she was tuned into the core issues I was dealing with and the root causes. A few minutes later, I could feel a tangible shift, like a weight had been lifted and a new level of energy had been opened. Something was palpably different about me — and all of this in minutes, not months! I look forward to what's possible with her incredible work, and encourage anyone struggling with issues (especially the seemingly unsolvable ones) to experience this for themselves.

GARY RUSH – Anthony Robbins Business and Success Coach

For all my life I have been uncomfortable expressing love to the people closest to me. There has always been this resistance to express the one emotion that is the essence of our existence.

As a result, there has always been this hole in my life that I ignored and that has denied me the depth and richness of life I deserve. Sandra, in just three sessions, nailed what had happened in my past and knew what was preventing me from being the person I so desperately wanted to be. She has a rare gift and talent to pick up what the blocks are and how to resolve them. As a coach for Tony Robbins and with many mentors in personal development, I know for a fact that very few have this ability.

After working with her, I feel more at peace with myself and know that I am now on track to express and experience more love in my life.

DONNA STONEHAM – Ph.D., author of *The Thriver's Edge: Seven Keys to Transform the Way You Live, Love, and Lead.*

Sandra Biskind has a direct connection to deep spiritual wisdom, and an uncanny ability to uncover the blind spots and help clear the blockages that keep you from living your best life. I highly recommend the powerful transformational work and books that the Biskinds are bestowing on the world.

ALISON HORA – Professional Dive Instructor

To sift through my thoughts and find a completely different person than two days ago has brought me to a place of great appreciation, and Sandra, I need to thank you for this. For me, the amazement of your work is that my life's structure is still there; people didn't disappear. But, my deep emotions have changed. The shift that has taken place within me is unbelievable.

If I was asked two days ago if it were possible to be clear and free from such deep inner pain and confusion so quickly, my answer would have been no. I would not have been able to even imagine my way to this place that I am now at. In the mornings, I now wake with excitement for my life. My energy levels have been restored, and I am happy and so truly honored to have met you.

AMBER BRECH-HOLLINS – Special Events Photographer

One of the most important decisions I have ever made in my life was to work on a personal level with Sandra and Daniel. I have worked with them for more than eight years because doing this work shifts me from crisis point to a place of absolute relief and neutrality in a matter of minutes.

It has transformed my life on every level and in every part of my life dramatically, and continues to do so. Whether it be for me personally with something I'm working on, or in my relationships with my husband, children, work colleagues, family, and friends, or in my businesses, every area is enriched and improved.

I am forever grateful for the peace and joy that it brings me back to. For bringing me back to my true self. My true north. Thank you, Sandra and Daniel.

ROBERT HURST –Owner, Alchemy Consulting

To say I am passionate about the new and improved direction in my life would be an understatement. I feel like an i7 processor in a 386 world. I have used Jim Rohn, Tony

Robbins, Dennis Waitley, and many others over the last 30 years. Nothing I have ever done can compare to the breakthrough technology that I have been lucky enough to experience through Sandra and Daniel and their Ultimate Mind Shift™ program.

JAMES HOLLINS – Business Owner and Entrepreneur

WOW! Words almost can't do justice to the incredible work that Sandra and Daniel do. To be able to go from totally on edge, stressed, depressed, angry, and "over life," to feeling happy, content, aligned, powerful, strong, and "in love" with life again, all in the space of a 30-minute session — truly amazing! I really appreciate being me again.

ALISON QUEDLEY – Former publisher and editor, IN TOUCH magazine

The books in The CODEBREAKER PLATINUM Series are *amazing,* just like you both. It comes straight from the heart and is written so deceptively simply. I am sure that people reading it will absorb the words on a very deep level without even realizing the changes the words will be making in their lives! These are life-changing books for anyone who is in any pain and distress, as well as those who want to carry on their journey into the Divine Mind and Love.

Can't wait until I can hold *CODEBREAKER: Discover the Password to Unlock The Best Version Of You* in my hands and feel the power of healing that I know will affect many, many souls.

Thank you both for your dedication to humanity and for your ever-present, loving connection.

ALSO BY SANDRA AND DANIEL BISKIND

The CODEBREAKER PLATINUM Series

PEACE: *Power Up Your Life*

LOVE: *Ignite The Secret To Your Success*

AWARENESS: *Discover How Life Really Works*

COMING SOON

TRUST: *Cultivate True Confidence*

INTEGRITY: *Master Your Inner Strength*

NEUTRALITY: *Go Beyond Positive - Your Key To Freedom*

UNITY: *Connect The Dots To Ultimate Happiness*

MINDFULNESS: *Access Your Awesome Potential*

AWARENESS

DISCOVER HOW LIFE REALLY WORKS

SANDRA AND DANIEL BISKIND

Third in The CODEBREAKER PLATINUM Series

AWARENESS: Discover How Life Really Works

Contents

INTRODUCTION
The CODEBREAKER PLATINUM Series

*"The road to hell is paved with good intentions.
The highway to heaven is cleared by removing the
unconscious obstacles to their accomplishment."*

- Sandra and Daniel Biskind

Collectively, the evolution of our souls is accelerating the realization of the new human: awakened, enlightened, self-actualized, and whole. Welcome! This series is dedicated to empowering your transformation — to supporting your rapid change and profound inner growth.

More than at any other time in history, there is the emerging potential to make huge shifts in consciousness that can take humanity — and yes, individuals — into a whole new stratosphere of living with peace and love, awareness, confidence and trust, integrity and neutrality, and mindful oneness with one another and the cosmos.

The CODEBREAKER PLATINUM Series has been conceived and designed to empower you to become the best version of you. In the 19th century there was a powerful transformational movement in the U.S., known as The Great Awakening. Now, in the 21st century, there is emerging an even greater awakening. Unlike its 19th-century predecessor, which was religious in nature, this broader, deeper movement is global, and it is based in spirituality rather than religion.

Spirituality, to paraphrase Deepak Chopra, "is the domain of awareness where we experience values like truth, goodness, beauty, love, and compassion, and also intuition, creativity, insight, and focused attention."

Similar to the holographic nature of the universe — and the mind — this series presents a wholistic thought system in which every part is not only consistent with the whole, but it contains the essence of the whole. As we think of the universe as a consciousness hologram, so we think of this thought system as a True Self hologram. Each key word in the Master Password PLATINUM is a symbol for an attribute of your True Self. There is just one True Self, but we can look at it from different angles to focus on specific attributes.

Just as sex education differs from sex training, this series presents tools, techniques, and practices to be used for mind training — not just for education. To get the full benefit, they need to be practiced. Mastery always involves repetition and practice. Mastering your mind to become the best version of yourself is no different.

The presentation we intentionally use is not linear, but to borrow a metaphor from Kenneth Wapnick, it is symphonic. A theme is presented. It is then repeatedly elaborated with variations. Finally it returns home to the original theme or motif. Rather than simply moving from Point A to Point B, the progression (to use another of his metaphors) is like ascending a circular staircase. This affords not only the added perspective of height, but also the ability to look 360 degrees around, as well as up and down. This presentation is helpful in internalizing such a different thought system.

We have discovered that everyone is always operating by codes. We choose our codes by default or by design. Our choice of code either empowers and uplifts us, or it deepens the rut we find ourselves seeking to escape.

As Bruce Lipton says, "The character of our life is based upon how we perceive it . . . our beliefs control our bodies, our minds, and thus our lives . . . we can control our lives by controlling our perceptions." How do we control our perceptions? Our codes control our perceptions. And, with or *without awareness, we choose the code.*

We are all searching for the same thing. We all want peace, love, and joy. We all want to be happy. Happiness, health, and success are attained naturally when we change to the correct code and remove their obstacles.

Life can change instantly with the removal of unconscious blocks. One example is of an extremely successful career woman who had never been married and lived alone with her cat. She was still ever hopeful of finding complete resolution around an ongoing, emotionally incapacitating issue.

She had spent 40 years and hundreds of thousands of dollars trying to find peace. She had experienced an incestuous relationship with her father in her teens that continued to torment her and sabotage her personal life. During a private session, we discovered the core program stopping her from ever having the kind of intimate relationship she longed for.

Using the Quantum Neutrality process, we neutralized the program stemming from the event. The emotional charge dissipated, and together we transformed the negative pattern ruining her life. In just one session, she shifted from someone who was traumatized and afraid of never having a fulfilling and meaningful relationship to finally feeling peaceful and optimistic about her future. In a word, she was finally happy.

Daniel and I have both overcome many debilitating life challenges. To thrive in adversity, we had to find inner strength and personal power. It was the work we present in this series that helped us through the tough times, and brought us back into alignment with our True Selves. We kept course-correcting back into our hearts until peace and love were restored.

To experience the richness of life, of real love and authentic forgiveness, we first had to master our own minds in order to come to that place of peace and love.

Having reached that place inside ourselves, and having assisted thousands of people around the world to do likewise, we knew that the next step in living our life purpose was to write these books. We want to share the tools and gifts we have developed that transformed our lives to help you do the same.

More than encouragement, the books in The CODEBREAKER PLATINUM Series act as guides and mentors on your amazing journey from the head to the heart. For some, this series will provide stimulating new ideas. For others, it will provide confirmation that you are on the right track to everyday enlightenment.

You don't have to change your religious or spiritual beliefs for these books to weave miracles in your life. Remember, you are not alone. To varying degrees, we all face the same challenges. And depending on the software programs you are running in your unique human computer, and your choice of code, you will create different levels of emotional adjustment as you deal with those challenges.

No matter how daunting or overwhelming your circumstances may seem, just like Daniel and me (along with countless others), you can turn your life around.

As you read, absorb, and apply The CODEBREAKER PLATINUM Master Password, you will begin to retrain your mind and transform your emotions and your experience of life. Reconnecting with the love that you are will accelerate your soul's evolution into enlightenment and wholeness. This will in turn propel you into greater levels of inner peace, joy, happiness, success, and optimal health — and a closer connection to the divine within you.

The information in the next five sections is repeated in the beginning of all the books in this series. They are explanations of what we mean when we talk about ego mind, the Divine Mind, the True Self, inquiry, attunement, neutrality, and enlightenment. Rereading these sections is beneficial in so many ways. Each time you read them will deepen their value to you.

"When you are connected to your

True Self

you will feel an ocean of

peace, love, and joy

moving in you."

- Sandra and Daniel Biskind

A BRIEF EXPLANATION OF TERMS

Some concepts basic to our work include: Your True Self, Ego Mind Programs, Neutrality, The Divine Mind, Living a PLATINUM Life, and Non-Duality.

YOUR TRUE SELF is the perfection of who you really are, and awareness is an eternal expression of your True Self, which is whole and complete.

EGO MIND PROGRAMS are parts of your self-image that you've fabricated, as opposed to the perfection of your True Self. If you have an ego mind program in which you believe you cannot access or trust your higher awareness, you will then create situations that prove that. You can't help but sabotage   —   or shortchange   —   your career, your relationships, and your health when you believe your intuition is inaccessible and your higher awareness can't be trusted.

NEUTRALITY is a state in which you are free of belief and attachment. Neutrality's open-mindedness enables you to access higher awareness, free of bias, emotion, and prejudice. The state of empowered Neutrality is where your ego mind's thoughts and emotions no longer control you. Neutrality is essential to love, peace, and real freedom, and it is the prerequisite to enlightenment.

THE DIVINE MIND is the ever-expanding, infinite expression of pure love and joy that expresses itself deep within you when you are no longer held hostage by the ego mind, but are free and at peace. It is the source of true reality, in contrast to the ego mind, which is the source of false reality.

LIVING A PLATINUM LIFE means that you have the skills to remain neutral and empowered — to maintain a PLATINUM state of mind — regardless of circumstances. In a PLATINUM life you live the perfection that you really are, free of limiting beliefs and ideas — free of inner turmoil.

Your relationships become more stable; you feel happier and healthier, more vital and creative. With less useless mind chatter, you have a more balanced emotional life. You are in touch with the field of infinite possibilities.

With a PLATINUM state of mind, you are continually becoming the best version of you.

NON-DUALITY is the natural foundational state of awareness of the unity of subject and object. It is where we understand we are all connected, not only to each other, but also to our Source and to all life.

"We need to understand that
thoughts are tools.
Are we using them as
productively as we can?
Are our thoughts
serving us well,
or are we their victims?
It's up to us."

- Dr. Tom Morris

HOW TO USE
The CODEBREAKER PLATINUM Series

THE WORK: No matter where you are on your own mystical journey into the real world of infinite love, peace, joy, and true success, you can use these tools and techniques to begin or continue to realign yourself with the high frequencies of the Divine Mind Code.

FIRST AID: Use *AWARENESS: Discover How Life Really Works* as a mentor when you need help on any level. Focus your intention on receiving the guidance you need, open the book randomly, and the chapter or page you see will be what you need to read in that moment. Or, if you prefer, look at the contents pages and use higher awareness to select the appropriate section to help you instantly feel better.

THE DIVINE MIND CODE: Use this book as a way to attune yourself to the frequency of the Divine Mind Code — accessible through your wholistic consciousness, which incorporates the maximal range of the human mind. The CODEBREAKER PLATINUM books unlock and activate the Divine Mind Code allowing your True Self to express its innate attributes of Peace, Love, Awareness, Trust, Integrity, Neutrality, Unity, and Mindfulness — reconnecting you to your personal power.

POEMS: When a poem appears, take a deep breath and relax. Do not rush through it, but savor it. Each one has been deliberately chosen to catapult you into your heart and illuminate your soul, flicking the switch on the light within. As often as you can, join these high-frequency beings as they bare their God-drenched souls to you.

MEDITATIONS AND VISUALIZATIONS: Simple meditations will attune you to the frequency of the relevant quality in each book. Repeating them will also help create new neural pathways in the brain. Eventually, these pathways become the dominant thought-processing pathways that help raise your level of awareness. Download your free meditations at www.TheBiskinds.com.

THE TOOL KIT: Simple three-point "keys" give you a fast and easy way to receive and assimilate information. Read and contemplate them repeatedly until they become like short passwords themselves. They will simply and effectively unlock your life code -- which accesses your personal power.

REPROGRAMMING THE BRAIN: Training the brain via repetition is also an essential way for you to learn. As you create new habit fields in the mind, they become reflected as new neural pathways that change the way the brain functions. The teachings will be repeated in short stories, metaphors, and analogies that repeat the same points in different contexts. Override your ego mind's voice when it tells you, "I have heard this all before."

As one of my teachers in Australia said, *"Because I love you so much, I will continue to give you the same information until you are living it."*

To maximize their transformational effect in your life, it is important not only to read these books often but also to immerse yourself in them — using the practices daily.

MAP OF AWARENESS

In our decades of experience in the art and science of personal transformation, we have helped thousands of people around the world, from London and New York to Los Angeles and Australasia. In our ongoing research and development, we discovered the Master Password that unlocks the Divine Mind Code for us. It was a fascinating process that revealed a code of such depth that we missed its power at first.

We took our time, as we are inviting you to do. As you begin to work with this secret password, multiple uses will be revealed for each concept. People who have read these books three and four times have said that the books became even more useful, insightful, and life-changing the more they read them.

We created a Map of Awareness inspired by the Hawkins scale of consciousness from the book *Power vs. Force: The Hidden Determinants of Human Behavior* by David Hawkins, M.D., Ph.D.

The Hawkins scale is two-dimensional, measuring consciousness in a vertical line going from 0 to 1,000, with 0 being the lowest state of consciousness. The majority of people are either 200 or below, and they are firmly entrenched in ego mind thinking. No one at this level of consciousness would even consider picking up, let alone reading, *AWARENESS: Discover How Life Really Works* or any of The CODEBREAKER PLATINUM Series.

Hawkins calibrated Einstein's consciousness at 499, which he considered the pinnacle of intellect. At 500, your heart opens and you begin to operate out of love. The state of unconditional love begins at 540. Enlightened states calibrate from 600 to 1,000, the theoretical maximum sustainable in a human body. Humanity's greatest masters, including Buddha and Jesus, calibrated at 1,000.

The Integrated Wholeness Scale is three dimensional and logarithmic. It adds a horizontal axis that measures personality issues that need to be resolved as you move from one level of awareness to another. Life challenges can trigger negative emotional responses and an infinite range of associated issues. As you move farther along both consciousness and personality sides of the scale together, the way you deal with them becomes more efficient and effective.

Unpacking personality programs from consciousness helps us to understand how high-consciousness people can do otherwise inexplicably low-consciousness deeds.

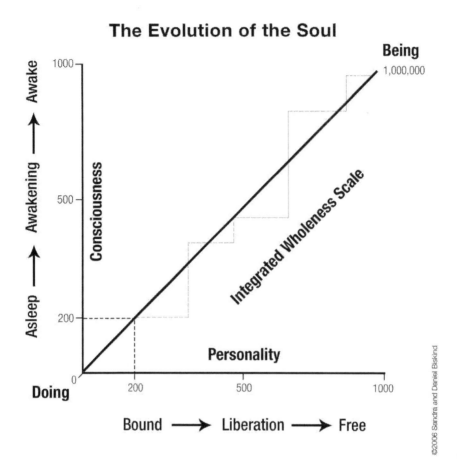

The CODEBREAKER PLATINUM Series presents a lifelong process of revelation, mastery, and ongoing practice and training. The immense power and beauty of your True Self is revealed increasingly with every book in the series. The words you are about to read will guide you into the mystical world of the Divine Mind – where you can no longer be held hostage in the fantasy world of your ego mind.

Join us on this journey to explore the non-dual world that is the home of your True Self.

THE MASTER PASSWORD

Here is The CODEBREAKER Master Password:

PEACE LOVE AWARENESS TRUST
INTEGRITY NEUTRALITY UNITY MINDFULNESS

PLATINUM is the Master Password that in the correct combination unlocks the secret to the Divine Mind Code for each of us.

This Master Password is like a key that awakens your consciousness and liberates your personality. As Buddha said, *"Your mind is everything. What you think, you become."* You can train your mind, be accountable for your soul choices, attune yourself to the Divine Mind Code, and ascend the Integrated Wholeness Scale into enlightened states.

PLATINUM unlocks the code to the inspiring, uplifting, true stories of the heart rather than perpetuating the deceptive, destructive, fictitious stories of the ego mind. This series presents a plan that makes your soul's choice to live by the wisdom of the Divine Mind Code — rather than the dictates of the ego mind code — a whole lot easier.

You can easily discover the passwords to your ego mind codes, and in doing so reveal the truth that you have been compromised and corrupted by the enemy within — the ego mind.

Some of them go something like this: paranoid, lost, attack, threat, intolerant, negative, unforgiving, malicious.

These words are below 100 on both the consciousness axis and personality axis of the Integrated Wholeness Scale.

PLATINUM acknowledges that you are already perfect, and that you are far more than the mere sum of your automated programs, conditioned thinking, and mindless self-talk. And, as you so well know, you are much more than what your physical senses reveal. You are a PLATINUM being. This is your True Self. Most people never realize this because their soul is asleep. They sleepwalk through life. Activating the PLATINUM password awakens your soul to choose wholeness again.

Learn to use the password to decode your life and break through to great loving relationships, real strength, and vitality — and the work and financial success you deserve.

Make the commitment to start living your PLATINUM life today.

As you read, absorb, and implement these concepts, you will retrain your mind, which transforms your experience of life. Accelerate your soul's journey into enlightenment and wholeness, and propel yourself into greater levels of love, joy, inner peace, happiness, better health, and a closer connection to the divine perfection within you.

Uh oh! What do I have to give up to live a PLATINUM life?

Sex, wine, shopping, credit cards . . . just kidding! Seriously, you will only be giving up your illusions and stories. You won't miss any of the things you have to give up to live a PLATINUM life, but you will naturally feel better, your light will shine brighter, and you will attract more love in your life. And, you will have loads more fun.

You have no doubt already learned that you can think positively about what you desire until you are blue in the face, but that does not mean those positive thoughts will manifest as changes in your life. Ultimately, your unconscious programs and patterns are running the show. Until those are corrected, your ability to manifest your best intentions will continue to be sabotaged by programs hidden in your unconscious mind.

Your life is a masterpiece in the making. You are here to evolve, become whole, and have fun. Let us help you fulfill your purpose by changing the inner landscape of your life, so that the outer landscape of your home, your work, and your relationships can reflect the change you want to be and see.

"When love and skill work together,

expect a masterpiece."

— John Ruskin

Ego Mind Code

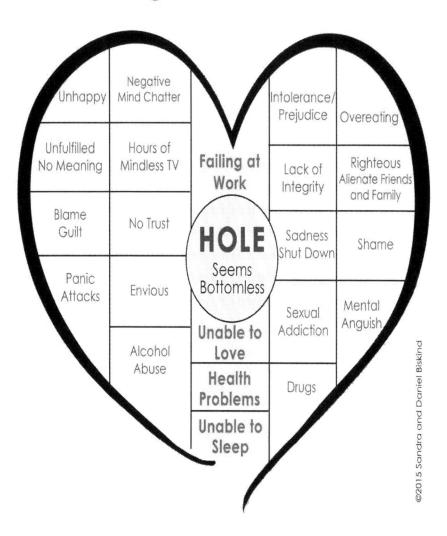

Divine Mind Code
Leads to Living a PLATINUM Life

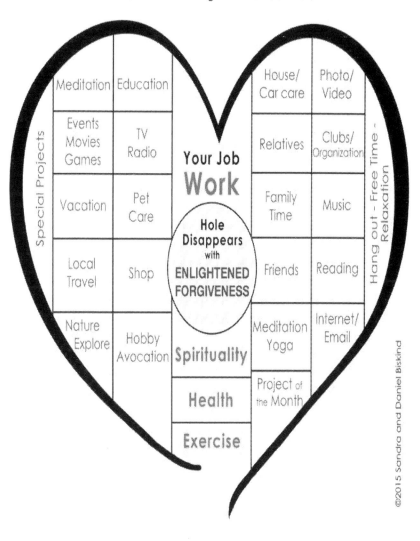

Living a PLATINUM Life

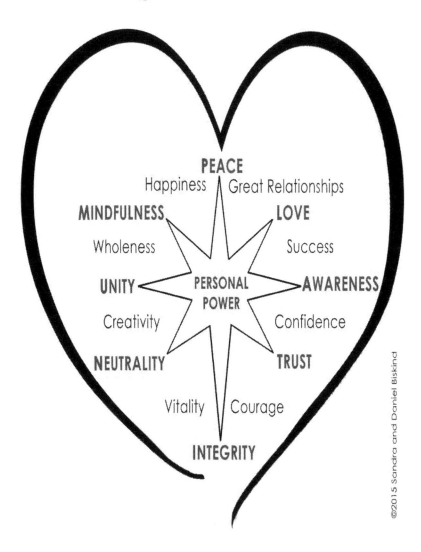

The CODEBREAKER PLATINUM Series presents groundbreaking concepts that will empower you to move into new levels of peace, love, and awareness, which lead to whole new ways of being. The aim of this system is for you to have a complete mind shift. That is why we call the process The Ultimate Mind Shift™.

This series has been intentionally designed to attune you to the supercharged frequency of enlightenment. You could feel very high, and sometimes your brain could feel heavy, because the energy field created as you read these books reconnects you to the enlightenment frequency. Its vibrational field, including the superconscious frequency of higher awareness, extends far beyond that of the conscious and unconscious minds. As your brain processes them, you may experience new and different sensations.

Use The CODEBREAKER PLATINUM password to crack the Divine Mind Code and start living the life of your dreams. As you read through these books, and as you pick up and implement the Key Passwords one at a time and put them together, you will create your own version of the extravagantly rich and beautiful life presented to you in this process of everyday enlightenment.

To maximize the transformational impact in your life, it is important not only to read these books often, but also to immerse yourself in them and to use the tools on a daily basis.

Here is what you will get from reading *AWARENESS: Discover How Life Really Works,* and from using the Ultimate Mind Shift™ teaching and training process:

- Increase your emotional intelligence, identify problematic habitual emotional responses to conflict in your life, and implement a powerful new strategy to resolve them while keeping peace of mind.
- Develop a strong, unwavering relationship with your

True Self and an ability to understand and utilize your higher awareness when making decisions in your everyday life.

- Receive energy that supports you and helps you love and feel loved and understood, regardless of conditions in your external world. Create new patterns and habits that support your health and well-being.

- Create the deep and lasting relationship of your dreams with your partner or future partner.

- Experience deeper love and connection, and better communication, with the people in your life.

- Become more energetically attractive and magnetic.

- Discover deeper meaning and purpose in your life.

- Delete old sabotage programs to free you to be more creative.

- Lead through love as you access your real power and strength.

- Master your inner critic and silence the chatter of your ego mind.

- Strengthen your connection to your spiritual core to live in a calm and balanced place, no matter what life throws at you.

- Experience an energetic frequency that regenerates, rejuvenates, strengthens, and renews every cell in your body.

- Access the mystical world of the Divine Mind, which automatically brings your body, mind, and soul into higher levels of awareness.

- Master the simple tools that progressively build a deeper and more sustainable connection to the PLATINUM password, the Divine Mind Code, and all of the attributes of your True Self.

- Attain a level of happiness that will astonish and delight you.

Have fun! And remember,

The secret to enlightenment is to lighten up!

WHAT IS ENLIGHTENMENT?

Enlightenment is the state in which you are fully connected to your True Self, often characterized by causeless love and limitless joy.

It is the state where you experience the world without projecting judgment.

Enlightenment empowers you to accept the perfection in everyone, and love them without reservation or condition.

It is the peaceful, confident experience of life, unfiltered by the programs of your ego mind. In enlightenment, the world is simply a mirror of you and the divine energy within you.

"It isn't by getting out of the world that we become enlightened, but by getting into the world...by getting so tuned in that we can ride the waves of our existence and never get tossed because we become the waves."

- Ken Kesey

Like many people, have you ever thought, *I don't want to be enlightened and live alone high on a mountain top, laughing at the rest of the world?* After a lifetime's desire to know, understand, and live an enlightened life, both Daniel and I have discovered that *that* is not what enlightenment is about at all.

I was fortunate to have spent many years working with an enlightened spiritual teacher who visited Melbourne a few times a year. I had just taken a seat when I realized the whole auditorium was full of an intense, iridescent purple light. Where was it coming from? I had been putting on stage shows for many years and had often used lighting technicians for special effects. No matter where I looked, I could not find the banks of lights that would have been needed to fill the whole room with this gorgeous wash of colored light.

I asked the person sitting beside me if he knew why our teacher was using purple light, and could he see where the light was coming from? He looked at me quizzically and said in an are-you-for-real voice, "What purple light? There's no purple light on the stage, or in the room." Well, there was purple light in the room *I* was sitting in! In exasperation, I closed my eyes. The same purple light was flooding my internal world.

So that's where it was coming from — inside me! I was the source of light. When I asked, the teacher told me the purple light I was seeing was my own spirit. Obviously, I could see this light with my physical eyes, but who was seeing it when my eyes were closed? It was my soul — the observer — that part of me that can never die and that is capable of fully connecting to my True Self. Like my physical eyes, my spiritual eyes were observing and relaying messages to the brain to process.

I had been working with this spiritual master for over six years, and in that time, I had changed the way I lived my life. I was meditating on a daily basis, and still working with other amazing healers and teachers, to hone my own ability to be the best version of myself.

I realized that I now coped with life challenges with more ease and less drama, and I was capable of being even more creative, more loving, and more forgiving than ever. And, I was totally addicted to the high of enlightenment. Feelings of joy and love would overwhelm me for no reason at all. I would see total strangers and be in love with all of them — no matter what they looked like. If this was an enlightened state, I wanted more.

During a public session with an Indian guru who was visiting Melbourne, a few hundred people were all invited to come to the front of the room for a hug with this enlightened being. I waited in line for over half an hour. (I would have waited even if I had been the last person in line — and it was a very long line.) When she held me in her arms close to her chest, she just said, "More. More. More." That became my mantra. More love, more joy, more wonder and fulfillment. If this was an enlightenment state and being connected to my Divine Mind, I was on the right path.

In the enlightened state, you understand the great mysteries of life, including that the whole of humanity is one wonderful idea, from the mind of God, which is manifesting in 7.3 billion unique ways. From an enlightened perspective, you understand that humanity has been hoodwinked into believing what the ego mind has told us — that we are separate from everyone else and need to look outside ourselves for the love, joy, success, health, and well-being that we seek.

Enlightenment is your natural state, and your thoughts are the only thing stopping you from having the life you want.

– Sandra Biskind

WHAT IS AWARENESS?

With awareness you intuitively see beyond ego mind stories and understand the big picture.

AWARENESS is beyond the realm of the ego mind.

The ego mind code can only operate in your unconscious and conscious states. It disconnects you from your True Self's higher awareness, so you remain separate, clueless, and dependent solely on the ego mind.

Higher awareness automatically gets the big picture and can see the forest — not only the trees. Your imagination, creativity, and intuition thrive when your soul chooses higher awareness, which is the harmonious integration of super-consciousness, everyday consciousness, and unconscious states. This is the key to virtual omniscience.

With Divine Mind awareness, you know you are part of a unified field of information and energy. You naturally intuit the right thing to say and do, for the highest and best good of all concerned.

Divine Mind awareness operates according to Quantum Field Theory, in which everything is interconnected.

That part of your being that is connected to the Divine Mind field has the capacity for virtual omniscience. It is capable of an infinite range of seemingly magical and mysterious feats. But they are only mysterious to the ego mind, for on the level of the Divine Mind, access to all knowledge is available to everyone.

"Not everything that can be

counted counts.

Not everything that counts

can be counted."

– Albert Einstein

CODEBREAKER SECRETS FOR SUCCESS: AWARENESS

The more aware you become, the more you realize there is more to life than what the ego mind and your physical senses present to you.

- Higher awareness is a cornerstone to having a successful, happy, and fulfilled life.

- Ego mind awareness is Newtonian, and it is totally invested in the physical world. The unconscious programs that were created during times of emotional stress will always subvert and stop your expansion into higher awareness.

- Divine Mind awareness operates according to Quantum Field Theory, in which everything is interconnected. It posits that even the simple act of looking at something — not to mention how you look at it — changes it on an atomic and subatomic level. Let's take it one step further: the very act of thinking about someone or something changes them or it.

- Knowledge is of the Divine Mind; perception is of the ego mind.

*"Your time is limited, so don't waste it
living someone else's life.
Don't be trapped by dogma - which is
living with the results of other
people's thinking.
Don't let the noise of others' opinions
drown out your own inner voice.
And most important, have the
courage to follow your
heart and intuition."*

– Steve Jobs

ACCESSING AWARENESS AND DIVINE INTERVENTION

"No, God — you've made a big mistake this time! I couldn't marry him. He's so thin I wouldn't be able to sleep with him. He'd hurt!"

Let's back up for a moment. I was conducting a meditation evening in Auckland at my manager's home. He came in from a doctor's appointment, and told everyone an American named Daniel Biskind, who had recently relocated to Auckland, was coming to tonight's session.

I asked him how he knew this man, and he said he didn't. At his first appointment with his new osteopath the day before, the doctor had told him he felt led to tell him about another patient, a man from the USA who had settled in New Zealand and who seemed very spiritual. My manager immediately told him he had a friend visiting from Australia who did life-changing work. Daniel happened to be coming in for an appointment with the osteopath later that same day, and Rob, my manager, asked the doctor to relay an invitation to him to join us the following evening.

When the osteopath told him that he was invited to a meditation session the next night, Daniel said he was aware of a voice inside his head saying, "Be there." The next night, which was to become a momentous occasion, my manager announced to the room that a man named Daniel Biskind was coming. Two women who had dropped in just to say "hi" immediately decided to stay. They had other plans for the evening, but at the mention of Daniel's name they changed their plans. They asked if they could stay, and then asked if they could use the bathroom to put on some makeup and freshen up.

While sitting on a bar stool at the kitchen bench with a huge smile on my face, I was thinking, "How cute is that." These two 45-year-old women had just morphed into excited 16-year-olds, and it was not because of my meditation session. It was because a new man was arriving who was interested in spirituality and personal transformation. Yes, a very sexy trait! My amusement didn't last long, though, for as soon as that thought had finished, I got the unequivocal message from spirit, "He's for you." I immediately went into shock and answered just as adamantly, "Oh no! I am not going to marry a man I have not even met."

I continued to object. "I have my family, my business, my house, my car, my cat, and my boyfriend in Australia, and I am not going to move to New Zealand." However, I did decide to go to the bathroom and put on some makeup.

When Daniel arrived, he handed my manager a cigar and a bottle of red wine. Well, that was that. My manager was over the moon and liked him immediately. The next person Daniel saw was me. He took one look at me, felt an inexplicable sense of recognition, and got another message from the same voice he had been aware of the previous day. It said, "Caution, caution, caution," which he loosely translated as meaning, "Be careful, this woman could rearrange your life."

You already know my response. Daniel had been on a vegan diet for over twelve months, and his bony body was thinly disguised under his clothes. His hair stuck straight up all over his head, and he had on the thickest glasses I had ever seen. I must confess, being experienced in transformation and design, I did do a quick and dirty assessment of how I could change his presentation.

It was time to ignore the message and get on with the night. I made the decision to stay as far away from him as possible. It was a really powerful evening, especially when a young child asked me how to handle an awkward situation with two of her friends. She was a very aware young girl of ten who felt sad when one of them had given her an ultimatum that day: choose between her and the other girl.

Through tears she said, "I don't want to choose. I love them both. What should I do?" Her eyes widened and the tears stopped as I told her there was room in her heart for both girls. She did not have to choose between loving one or the other, but could choose to love them both. She didn't have a problem with either girl, and she could easily work out a way to see them at different times. Awareness dawned. Her ten-year-old smile lit up the room as she said, "I do love them both. I am so happy! I thought I only had one choice and that meant I would lose one or even both of them."

After the session, everyone was invited to stay for pizza and a glass of wine. The two women who had put their makeup on said they had to go. I wanted them to stay. I was fighting my own divine guidance, once again, but when I asked them to consider staying to spend more time with Daniel, they smugly replied, "We don't want to seem too keen too soon. We live here, so we can make a time to catch up with him next week."

If they had been more aware and listening to their intuition, it would have told them this was it — it's now or never. In the effort to appear cool and play the relationship game, they had just lost their one opportunity to talk to Daniel and create a connection. Daniel, on the other hand, was not playing games — he was playing for keeps. He was tapped in to his awareness, and he immediately followed his inner guidance to turn up for an evening of meditation that was so much more than that.

He also knew his whole life was about to change. At one o'clock in the morning, when everyone else had left or gone to bed, Daniel was not going anywhere. He was about to put on more music and open another bottle of wine when I exclaimed, "Hey, what are you doing?" I told him I was tired and he had to go home. He looked at me (to all the men reading this, are you listening?) and said, "There are certain times in your life when you come across something so special you don't want to leave it, not even for sleep."

WOW! I hope you are taking notes here. This was really good stuff. I was very impressed and told him that was definitely worth ten points, but he still had to leave. Very earthy Aussie, I'm afraid. Two nights later, after dinner with a small group and after telling his accountant the day before he wasn't sure if he was ready for this, by which he meant me, Daniel made the best marriage proposal I have ever heard. (This was only our second time in each other's presence.)

It was late again, and I was leaving for Australia the next morning. Every cell in my whole body had been shaking for hours because I knew Daniel was going to ask me to marry him that night. It was deja vu from the meditation night, except this time he said, "I want to take you home and look after you for the rest of your life." Well, that was even better than anything he had said on our first meeting — and that had been brilliant.

So many people had used their awareness to make this meeting happen. My manager had intuited which doctor to go to, and had not been at all upset or even surprised when his new physician talked to him about wanting to make an introduction to another one of his patients. In fact, being very aware, he accepted it as quite normal.

The doctor had accessed his innate awareness to know he was supposed to introduce these two patients, something he normally would never even have considered. Daniel was definitely connected to his spiritual core and following his inner guidance, his higher awareness. I was the only one who was bucking, kicking, and screaming to myself that this could not be happening, even though my super-consciousness told me it was a done deal.

I had my life sorted, and I was in a great place emotionally, mentally and spiritually. Or so I thought. The divine guidance I had followed and fought with since my childhood had different ideas, and it was once again throwing out dictates that were hard to ignore.

Daniel took me to the airport the next day and gave me a warm and innocent hug goodbye. When I got back to Australia, I drove straight to my spiritual mentor's home, and in the safety of her cozy, familiar room, I proceeded to tell her nothing. I was still in shock, and as it turns out, only minutes later, so was she. She looked at me and said, "I don't care who you have been hugging, he's not for you!"

"Phew!" I thought. I was off the hook. As it happened, right in that moment, my then 83-year-old best friend and spiritual mentor knew I was going to leave Australia and marry this man. She was so tuned into her superconsciousness that she was also aware it was a done deal. She did not want me to leave, and she was deliberately trying to avert what to her was this looming disaster.

When I saw my boyfriend next, I told him I had met an American man in New Zealand, and before I could finish the sentence, his awareness had kicked in with the internal message, "It's over." Daniel later told me that when I explained I had a partner in Australia, he also got the identical inner guidance, "That's over."

There is so much more to this story, but needless to say, here we are, sixteen years later, and closer than ever. No matter how hard I resisted and fought my destiny as shown to me through inner knowing, divine guidance, and higher awareness, it was never going to do any good. My life, too, was to be rearranged. I had been arguing with these divine beings for as long as I could remember, and as it turned out — surprise, surprise — as always, they were right.

The long chain of amazing events in this story not only heightened my state of awareness, but it also depended on my utilizing an expanded range of consciousness. This provided a better road map to guide me, especially where added attention and effective communication were high priorities. I was acutely aware of the feelings and thoughts of the people around me. Most were positive and even joyous, but there were definitely some in which the ego mind code was dominant, rendering the ground soft and even potentially dangerous.

The more you facilitate your soul's evolution, the more your higher awareness helps you negotiate life challenges and achieve more success.

KNOW YOUR AUDIENCE

Here is a wonderful true story a friend of ours tells about an event he was responsible for as the president of the Chamber of Commerce of Northeastern Ohio — the largest metropolitan chamber in the United States.

The event was the Chamber's annual meeting. The scheduled speaker was the CEO of Cleveland's corporate icon — one of the world's largest corporations, which was based in the UK. There was a sell-out of 1,700 seats in record time. Three days before the event was to take place, our friend received a call from the White House. The representative of the President of the United States explained that the President wanted to attend the Chamber's annual meeting to announce one of his major initiatives for the coming year.

During the next 60 minutes, the proverbial 'herding cats' would have seemed orderly compared to what actually happened. The Fortune 100 CEO who was to speak was given the news immediately. He was a man of great integrity, and he jokingly remarked that it would be the first time that he would have the privilege of serving as the warm-up speaker for the President of the United States. Obviously, this was now a new ballgame! On a scale of 1 to 100, it would be a coup somewhere north of 1,000. Predictably, the media went wild.

The White House staff and the Chamber's marketing people explained that media from across the nation would attend, requiring a minimum of 200 seats. That was not the worst of the seating problems. Television media would require a high-vantage platform that would circle the room, about three-quarters of the way from the front. This resulted in some 400 ticket holders being blocked off from sight of the podium and speakers. Our friend quickly scheduled another room that was off at an angle to the main room.

On the day of the event, it didn't take too much awareness to know that his relocated guests were unhappy about their seating arrangements. When his illustrious guest speaker arrived, our friend explained the problem to him. The President, aware of the need for everyone to have a great experience, asked if it would help if he "worked" the adjoining room. "Oh," said our friend, "it would probably just save my job, Mr. President!"

With a smile and a pat on the back, the President headed straight for the smaller room. He then proceeded to personally shake hands with every person in the area and to chat at each table. Then the President walked through the main room, past everyone seated there, and onto the stage to present his plan in his keynote address.

The formerly disgruntled people in the side room no longer felt unhappy or disadvantaged. To the contrary, they were the ones who got bragging rights to having spent personal time with the President of the United States. This is a great example of how a problem was turned into a huge success by two people who knew where added attention was needed, and where communication was a high priority. No wonder that to this day, our friend names that president as his favorite of all time.

You can access your own version of everyday awareness whenever you observe with empathy a smile or frown, or a greeting that's warm or cool. You do not have to be accessing higher awareness to understand the needs of others and how you can best serve them. Think of times you have been successful at work, completed a difficult project, or placated a disgruntled person. What do you think you did in order to find the solution to any of these problems? You used your awareness to tap in to the needs of the people and the situation to mold a desirable outcome.

Virtually all successful people have found a way to access higher awareness — even if only in a narrow application to their field of specialization. Sooner or later, they almost all acknowledge the importance of higher awareness. They may describe it as intuition, or a gut feeling, or an inner knowing — but however they describe it, it is higher awareness.

"There is a universal, intelligent life force that exists within everyone and everything. It resides within each one of us as a deep wisdom, an inner knowing. We can access this wonderful source of knowledge and wisdom through our intuition, an inner sense that tells us what feels right and true for us at any given moment."

— Shakti Gawain

VIRTUAL OMNISCIENCE

When you are accessing your superconscious dimensions of higher awareness, you have virtual omniscience, which is the ability to access the relevant information you need at the moment — on the spot. This is how life really works.

Have you ever seen people totally enrapt with a speaker, or with someone who is talking to them? The awareness of high-consciousness people is magnetically attractive to others. In a case like this, the speaker is highly aware of his or her audience and attuned to their shifting needs and nuances. Any successful speaker will tell you that being tapped into higher awareness allows them to feel and know if they have lost their audience and, with that knowledge, they can get the conversation back on track. Successful teachers, mentors, business people, and others who work with people — and yes, especially successful presidents — constantly employ their awareness to know how to handle any situation with anyone.

Being mindful of how you are feeling in any given moment and being able to get neutral to anything upsetting your alignment with your True Self is only half of the success equation.

Being aware of how other people are feeling, and then knowing how to interact with your family, friends, co-workers, and the rest of the world is the other half.

In Lynne McTaggart's book *The Field,* she talks about a band of scientists who have gone beyond conventional quantum theory. Through research and thinking outside known boxes, they discovered that due to a vast quantum field, or Zero Point Field — the energy field that is the very underpinning of our universe — none of us are in fact alone.

We are all connected. There is a unity to humanity and, indeed, to the entire cosmos.

With higher awareness — specifically, superconsciousness — you can access information from anywhere and anything in the field. This is very good news for humanity, but not so good for the untrained ego mind.

I worked with a powerful CEO of a successful executive-leadership consulting firm who was about to step onto the world stage with her latest best-selling book and media tour. During the session, she confided she was feeling overwhelmed and anxious. Even with the support of her staff, she felt like she was juggling so many things she couldn't keep up.

When working with clients, individually or in a group, I am tuned in to my superconscious higher awareness and the Zero Point field. Some people call this accessing the Akashic records, but in reality it is more than that. As I tuned in for our heroine, a small child of only four appeared to me. With tears running down her face, this little one proceeded to tell me how she was being used and abused by her father in that lifetime. Ashamed and grief stricken, the child told me she needed to hide and stay small and not draw any attention to herself. Her ego mind created a number of programs that became her beliefs from that day forward. Both the small child and my client were living by an unconscious ego mind code that was sabotaging my client's success, not only in the business world, but also in her personal relationships.

The code ran like this: Being beautiful is dangerous. Standing out is dangerous. Don't draw attention to yourself, ever.

People who love you hurt you.

I described this little girl and relayed what the she was telling me to our heroine. Astonished, she said she knew this little one very well because it was her story in this lifetime, too. Both the small child's programs from her past life and her little one's programs from this life needed to be corrected so she could be neutral to the emotions around these events. Using the Quantum Neutrality process, I dissolved the emotional charge around the events and deleted their effects, which instantly changed her code. After energetically placing a forgiveness template into her heart, she was then able to step into the freedom of forgiveness.

Our heroine had started the session feeling overwhelmed and anxious at the prospect of launching herself into the world on a larger scale. However, with absolute amazement and relief in her voice, she said she could no longer even find what she had been anxious about in the first place.

There was no way my client would have equated what had happened to her 40 years ago to the struggles and challenges she was having now. The codes allowed her to create a successful business — but only up to a point. Two weeks before our appointment, a fight with her brother had triggered the program, and life became an ominous and threatening place once again.

After being set free from these unconscious programs, our heroine felt as though she could easily handle what needed to be done. She was confidently looking forward to stepping into her greatness: to inspire, uplift, and empower her clients and audience. Even after spending years in therapy and believing she was free from her childhood traumas, it had required higher awareness and the Quantum Neutrality process to finally free her to be seen, to be heard, to love and be loved — to be truly successful.

Learning to tap into your own virtual omniscience is the key to breaking the codes that keep you from your greatness, from living aligned with your True Self. Use the Quantum Neutrality process, whenever something triggers a sabotage code, to instantly course-correct back into your personal power.

When you feel any version of fear, negativity, and pain, you know an ego mind code has been triggered. Identifying the responsible core program by using higher awareness is what we do in the Quantum Neutrality process. We teach and train this, and we use it in our work (and in our daily lives) all the time — and you can, too.

To learn more about the Zero Point Field and the scientific background for virtual omniscience, here is some suggested reading. Daniel and I are drawn to reading and learning about the latest discoveries in science, not only for the content, but also because we enjoy the exuberance and creativity of the high consciousness coming out of the pages. Have fun with these incredible books. Like The CODEBREAKER PLATINUM Series, the information and energy in them will open your mind and literally change your level of awareness as you read them:

Lynne McTaggart, *THE FIELD: The Quest for the Secret Force of the Universe*, Harper Collins

Valerie V. Hunt, Ph.D., *INFINITE MIND: Science of Human Vibrations of Consciousness*, Malibu Publishing Co.

Bruce H. Lipton, Ph.D., *The BIOLOGY OF BELIEF*, Hay House, Inc. NY

THE POWER OF MIND FIELDS

"The mind, an energetic field of thought, is broadcasting fields. A new process called magnetoencephalography (MEG) reads the fields without even touching the body."

– Bruce H. Lipton, Ph.D.

Have you ever walked into a room after people have been fighting, grieving, or having a good time? Depending on your state of awareness, you can become instantly aware of the feelings of anger, sorrow, or joy. Depending on the frequencies still vibrating in the area — the mind field — you may feel as if you want to stay in that place or leave it. Everyone has experienced being aware of the leftover remnants of information from within the mind fields or human energy fields that we all continuously create.

On a gray and drizzly May day in London, Daniel and I had been walking the streets for hours, as only tourists do. By late afternoon, our feet were sore, our legs were tired, and we were ready for a break, when we came upon Westminster Abbey. It was a great place to sit, away from the bustle and constant noise of such a big city.

We had forgotten to take into account all the other tourists in the town, who all appeared to be in Westminster Abbey at the same time. The church was brimming with people from all over the world, every different race, color, and creed, each with their different levels of awareness, and none of them praying at the time.

Even with so many people present, there was a silence in this huge abbey that was magnified by the contrast of the slightest noise. As we wove our way through the surprisingly silent throngs of people, an extraordinarily beautiful-sounding bell rang three times. A clergywoman came out in full robes, stood at a lectern, and began to say a prayer.

Having been built on some of the earth's most powerful ley lines, many of these grand houses of worship were designed to enhance and amplify the inherent energy frequency of these sites, which had always been power places. We had already been picking up on the very palpable energy field of love and devotion that had built up over the centuries, but during this prayer, we became overwhelmed by the high frequency of divine devotion.

As tourists, we had visited many of the world's most beautiful churches and holy places without ever being lucky enough to experience this kind of seemingly spontaneous prayer. Our hearts leapt as we looked at each other in wonder and surprise at how blessed we were to be there in that moment. With tears threatening to spill from our eyes, we found a place to sit and just "be," in a state of joy, in the presence of that incredible energy field of love.

However, when we arrived at Ground Zero in New York, it was a totally different story. We were overwhelmed, and reduced to tears of sadness, by the mind field of grief that inhabited this site of destruction and death. It was all I could do not to break down and sob. It felt as though once I started, I could never stop.

This devastation was the result of the soul's choice, over millennia, to listen to the untrained ego mind. Operating in the ego mind code leads to unforgiveness, separation, religious dogma, the self-righteousness of fanaticism, and overt violence.

"Just as the subatomic particles

that compose us

cannot be separated from

the space and particles

surrounding them,

so living beings

cannot be isolated

from each other."

– Lynne McTaggart

SENSING CATASTROPHES WHEN THEY OCCUR

"The power of the human mind is such that we could monitor and decode all major "goings on" in the world. Without the news media, we could sense starvation and catastrophes when they occur."

– Valerie V. Hunt, Ph.D.

Do you remember where you were and what you were feeling on the morning of September 11, 2001? I will never forget. I awoke crying in a state of total devastation, and I felt as though my heart was breaking once again. It was 7:30 in the morning, New Zealand time. With concern, Daniel asked, "What's wrong? What's happened?" I told him I knew someone in my family had just died. It was too early to call Australia, so we decided to wait for a couple of hours to find out what tragic event had befallen someone I loved. Even if I had wanted to, my body would not stop crying. Feelings of loss and tragedy filled every cell of my being.

Our building site manager phoned us to ask if we had seen the news. He told us a plane had crashed into one of the Twin Towers in New York. We didn't believe him. "He must be joking." We turned on the news just in time to see another plane crash into the second tower. This incomprehensible act of terrorism had indeed killed a member of my family. Almost 3,000 members of my family, in fact. Even though I was on the other side of the planet, in a different time zone, and asleep at that, on a superconscious level I still connected with an event that literally rocked our world into sadness and disbelief.

Valerie V. Hunt, Ph.D., author of *Infinite Mind: Science of the Human Vibrations of Consciousness*, says, "The mind is a wireless transmitter and receptor. We acknowledge as commonplace that we can send and receive radio waves, bounce them off satellites, unscramble them, and materialize information transmitted over a distance. But, we still cannot accept that all the marvelous things we invent or discover 'out there' are really prototypes of the body and the mind field."

With these insights, she helps us unscramble and demystify our ability to be in many places at once and to know the news from the other side of the world without all our material devices. When that part of your being known as your superconsciousness is connected to the divine mind field you have the capacity for virtual omniscience. Superconsciousness is capable of an infinite range of seemingly magical and mysterious feats. But they are only mysterious to the ego mind.

On the level of Divine Mind, each of us can know all we need to know.

The Big Bang is the idea that we can be separate from our source, our creator — separate from God. After imagining that, which in the Old Testament corresponds to eating the apple from the Tree of the Knowledge of Good and Evil, the Bible goes on to say that Adam (like us) fell into a deep sleep. And (again like us) nowhere does it say that Adam ever woke up.

In the dream state, this impossible idea grew quickly. Humanity found itself adrift in the ocean of an unconscious dream, no longer neutral and no longer whole. It did not take long before the illusory world in this sleep state became "real" to us. In our deep sleep, the dream continues to build form and substance. The untrained ego mind defends duality to the death in order to perpetuate this dream state — and itself.

Your ego mind has created almost unbreakable codes that it convincingly brainwashes you into thinking are meant to keep you safe. But neither it nor its codes can do that. They are not real.

As science, technology, and spirituality converge, more people are deciphering these life codes and moving into higher levels of awareness. Only there are you truly safe. Only there can you experience pure love.

Your soul, in its journeys into the unknown, has mistakenly made the choice to listen to this primitive mind — instead of the Divine Mind — and it has done this so often that it now believes the tales of the ego mind to the exclusion of the Divine Mind.

The primitive ego mind's number-one priority is for you not to wake up. Your realization that it exists only in your sleep state in a fantasy world of its own creation can be its undoing. When no longer ignored and trampled by an unaware split mind, the Divine Mind can at last come in from the imaginary cold.

Only your soul can choose between the asleep ego mind and the awake Divine Mind. In the awakening process, you journey from the dream to a lucid dream to finally waking up. Bring out the champagne!

Tripping Over Joy

What is the difference
Between your experience of Existence
And that of a saint?

The saint knows
That the spiritual path
Is a sublime chess game with God

And that the Beloved
Has just made such a Fantastic Move

That the saint is now continually
Tripping over Joy
And bursting out in Laughter
And saying, "I Surrender!"

Whereas, my dear,
I am afraid you still think

You have a thousand serious moves.

- Hafiz, (Translated by Daniel Ladinsky)

From the Penguin publication I Heard God Laughing: Poems of Hope and Joy.
Copyright 1996 & 2006 by Daniel Ladinsky and used with his permission

THE LIFE OF PI IN 3D

You do not have to have seen the movie *The Life of Pi* in 3D to be able to use your imagination and put yourself in a lifeboat, where you sit stranded, in the middle of an ocean, in your unconscious dream. Even through the fear and uncertainty, you are overwhelmed by the beauty of the world around you. The striking colors of the rising and setting sun take your breath away. We are all addicted to the fantastic work of art that is our illusory world. However, both the awe you feel and the beauty around you are unstable. Like the ocean, everything is always changing.

This is without taking into account the danger that exists within your own life raft. Just as in the movie, you have a man-eating tiger that could bring death at any moment keeping you on your toes. As the tiger destroys everyone else in the boat, it becomes your one constant companion. Through hardship and the fear of dying, you come to love the tiger — this dark and dangerous force — as you journey together, weathering the storms of your sleep state. The ego mind is both the man-eating tiger and the changing weather conditions, and just as in your own Hollywood studio, it has you out there in the choppy waters of your sleep state, always making up ways to scare you to death.

Because a world without love would not be worth living in, the soul chooses to give the occasional bit part to the Divine Mind, your True Self, to play a small role in the dream world. However, the love that you are and always will be never leaves the set. It steadily whispers to gently awaken you from this deep and restless sleep.

One of my clients called me for a private session. She was in tears, hoping I could work with both her and her husband, as he was about to walk out the door and never come back. Since their delicious baby girl had been born, they had been miscommunicating for many months — and both had finally had enough. Every woman who has ever had a baby knows the upheaval and massive changes that take place both before and after her precious bundle arrives. And every man who has ever become a father knows exactly the same thing.

Even while love is present at the marriage ceremony, during the honeymoon, and for years to follow, the introduction of a child into any relationship creates not only a cause for celebration but also the need for careful communication.

We are all here in a body to do just that — communicate. What amazing communication devices our bodies are. They are pure energy, and they transmit the frequencies at which we are oscillating, out into the rest of the world. This goes beyond our five senses that seem to bind us to the illusory world of the ego mind.

This is your higher awareness. It routinely gets blindsided by the programs that are triggered when notable life events occur.

Have you ever felt as though you knew something, but didn't know how you knew it? Have you ever felt uncomfortable around someone, and didn't understand what was making you feel that way?

That's your sixth sense, or your higher awareness, in action. You are always picking up information from the human mind field, and you are always transmitting into it.

"It is the 'sixth sense' coming from the human field, the finest of all senses, which gives us the elaborate, distant knowledge about the happenings in the cosmosphere."

– Valerie V. Hunt, Ph.D.

My client said that she felt unloved and unappreciated by her husband. "When he comes home from work and takes one look at our baby girl, his whole face lights up. He doesn't look at me like that anymore. I can't stand it. He gives the baby and our oldest daughter more attention than he gives me."

Her husband (also a client) came on the phone, and he told me how angry he was because his wife always made him feel bad when he came home from a hard day's work by giving him what he called 'dirty looks.' Rather than look at her, he focused all his attention on the baby because she was the one who lit up in his presence, which made him feel full of joy.

They were both operating by ego mind codes. They were both out of alignment with their True Self. They were having a relationship crisis because they were not using higher awareness to sort out what was really going on. The ego mind code had them in their own separate life rafts, feeling alone, overwhelmed, and in danger. And of course, each blamed the other for the way they felt. In fact, they were both projecting their own man-eating tiger onto the other.

As I started to unravel the situation for them, they realized the man-eating tiger was not their partner, but indeed, their own ego mind.

The husband thought his wife was reacting badly to him because of historic events that had happened previously in their relationship. The wife was acutely jealous of the love he was giving to the baby and not to her. She simply wanted some of that love.

She was projecting her 'I'm not good enough' programs onto him, which manifested as jealousy. He was projecting his 'I'm not good enough' programs onto her, which manifested as feeling judged. That triggered anger and separation. Their codes were the perfect mirror image of each other. By neutralizing these programs and deleting their effects, I was able to assist them to quickly reawaken to the love that they are.

Have you ever been in a situation where you are blaming the man-eating tiger that you think is someone else for your own unhappiness?

But that is not how life really works.

HOW LIFE REALLY WORKS

Your ego mind programs are the changing weather conditions and the man-eating tiger that sabotage the best version of you every time. Using everyday awareness, you can quickly intuit something is wrong and then begin a process of communication — first with yourself and then with your partner.

Explain to them that you feel uncomfortable about a situation, and that you know something is not quite right. Something within you has been triggered by their behavior and you would like help finding out what it is.

Notice that you have not told them they are wrong, nor are you blaming them for your feelings.

You have told the truth. You are taking 100% responsibility for your feelings, emotions, and reactions. You are aware that you are out of alignment with your True Self.

If you are not feeling love, you have moved away from your perfect point of power, from the Divine Mind Code and the best version of who you are. It is in such moments that your life changes, and you find yourself firmly ensconced back in the illusory world of separation, guilt, shame, and blame. No longer aware of how life really works, you find yourself sleepwalking into your own unique version of a nightmare. Separation, divorce, heartache, and loneliness are normal when operating in the ego mind code. It shuts down your awareness and sabotages your relationships.

Be curious. Demonstrate the sexiest trait on the planet by becoming the best version of you and learning all you can about yourself and the people in your life, especially your partner. That knowledge could save your relationships — and even your life some day.

In her childhood, when my client's father left the family, she had felt abandoned. Either consciously or unconsciously, children inevitably blame themselves when parents divorce. That insidious 'I'm not good enough' program running quietly in the background in her unconscious mind had been triggered by her husband's behavior. Her ego mind jumped in with all its negative mind chatter, and began to blame him for her feelings of despair and loneliness.

Remember, separation is the ultimate victory for the ego mind.

Our heroine was totally unaware of the emotions and subsequent programs of the little girl within her — the child who had felt devastated, abandoned, and confused when her father left the family. As an adult, our heroine felt she was being abandoned all over again by her husband, who had pulled his affection away from her.

He was feeling guilt and shame over many issues from the past, and he perceived his wife's looks and behavior as disapproval rather than disappointment. In this case, our hero was in fact judging himself as wrong. He had not forgiven himself, and he was full of guilt and shame. Triggering an unforgiveness program toward himself, his projections made his wife judge and jury. It did not occur to him that her behavior had nothing to do with their past. Rather, it had everything to do with her 'I'm not good enough' program, which had been set off by feelings of lack of love and affection in the present moment.

It is easy to see how devious the ego mind is as it creatively keeps you asleep to your programs. All your programs are woven together so tightly that it can be hard to unravel them. By not taking yourself back to the love that you are, they constitute a reliable recipe for disaster.

After neutralizing and deleting all their relevant programs, I asked the couple to focus their awareness into their hearts, and remember all the love and wholeness they experienced the day they were married.

Then, from that place, I asked them to forgive their own and their partner's programs — not their partner. Did you get that?

This is how life really works.

You have a body whose job is to communicate with you and the cosmos. Your five senses work in conjunction with you in this wonder that is your life. It is always doing this, but are you always listening? Incorporate them, and then go beyond your five senses. Using the Divine Mind Code activates your higher awareness, your sixth sense, to stay connected with the cosmos and the information most relevant to you.

You have this ability. Your noble purpose in life includes evolving and growing your awareness so that in any given moment your soul's choice is the Divine Mind code. As you do this, your life becomes the magnificent creation you have always wanted it to be.

It is inappropriate to say that it's weird when your natural ability to use your awareness gives you a 'gut' feeling. It's hardly 'woo woo' when you use your powers of observation, discernment, and intuition to understand what needs to be said or done in any situation.

"Intuition is the only important thing."

— Albert Einstein

Once realigned with the higher awareness of their hearts, my clients were able to forgive both their own and their partner's programs. They easily recreated the energy field of love, and rather than walk out the door and leave love behind I had the distinct feeling they were off to make more babies.

We all have the choice to leave love behind, but why would we? It is only your unconscious, sleep-walking self that is trapped in the life raft of death and destruction. *You* are not!

Get yourself onto the level of love or above on the Integrated Wholeness Scale, which is truly a Map of Awareness. It is always all about you — your programs, your ideas, your stories, and your beliefs. Imagine what a wonderful world it would be if we all made the decision right now to diligently use our higher awareness to reconnect to the oneness of the human information field — and to use the heart to forgive and love, 100% of the time. This is called living by the Divine Mind code — which is living in a PLATINUM state of mind.

Daniel and I have made that commitment to love ourselves, each other, and you that way. What about you? It's your choice. Have you made that decision yet?

Love facilitates transformation.

Love is the fuel of miracles.

Love no matter what.

– Sandra and Daniel Biskind

PRIMITIVE MAN

As a matter of survival, in primitive times the soul continually chose the ego mind. It was obvious to our forefathers that they had to kill or be killed. Just like them and the man-eating tiger, the ego mind has always been a master killer. These choices were so effective in keeping the dream persona alive that the body and the brain naturally became trained in the art of war. The human experience of survival in this new frontier molded what you have come to know as the very nature of humanity. When you talk about human nature from this perspective, you are describing another construct of the soul's imaginary fall from grace.

Having mastered the art of killing, combined with the ego mind's natural tendency toward it, humanity evolved in our dream world into such an alien species that we have become unrecognizable, even to ourselves. Your ego mind's campaign for domination, not to mention its fight for its own survival, is ongoing. It attacks anything outside its frame of reference and will not hesitate even to kill anyone who threatens it. The soul's choices to create religions in an effort to get back to God have routinely been hijacked, and they often backfire. The devastation of September 11, along with every other war ever fought over religious beliefs and dogma, provide an inexhaustible supply of examples of this.

This dualistic system keeps the sleeping soul confused and off balance as it oscillates uncertainly between the choices of the lowest common denominator of the make-believe mind and the highest level of awareness, the Divine Mind.

We all know our history. The depths of darkness of the ego mind know no boundaries. Master of war and politics, the ego mind presents a convincing case to the soul to keep choosing it. Humanity's history of violence against those who tried to find their way into the light of wakefulness is the devastating story of souls who were not ready to move into the light. The result of their conquests is the world we live in today. Most religions became enmeshed in war, power, and politics. Spirituality was rejected in a frightening display that took the dream to nightmare status, especially for the mystics, healers, and those aspiring to live by the Divine Mind Code.

"When we quit thinking primarily

about ourselves and our own

self-preservation,

we undergo a truly heroic

transformation of consciousness."

- Joseph Campbell

LANDSLIDE INTO WAKEFULNESS

Even though the ego mind undermines and tries to subvert love's power to wake us up, many souls are ready to leave the confines of their illusory coma and move back into the safe haven of the Divine Mind.

Can you feel the pull of your soul toward happiness, love, and joy as you become more aware of the need to attend to your own soul's evolution?

At first a tentative move by the soul to change direction by changing its choices, it has now taken on the quality of a landslide into wakefulness. The only danger this landslide poses is to the part of the illusion that refuses to get out of the way. It has put up a great fight, and most souls are still not yet ready to give up the choice to remain in the illusory world.

However, help is on its way. All is never lost. Your True Self sits dutifully at the foot of the bed you have made for yourself. It never gives up on you and your return to life, to sanity, and to wakefulness. It is always poised to reassure you when you stir from your sleep that you are in the safe haven of the Divine heart — which you have never really left.

How much have you invested in your physical, intellectual, and emotional development? Aren't your enlightenment, your spiritual development, your awakening worth at least as much?

To develop a PLATINUM state of mind and live a PLATINUM life, you need to cultivate the spiritual aspects of your soul.

"Just as a candle cannot burn without fire, men cannot live without a spiritual life."

— *Buddha*

SPIRIT JUNKIE

*"When one represses emotion, one's body hurts;
when one represses consciousness, one's mind
hurts; when one represses spirituality,
one's soul suffers."*

– Valerie V. Hunt, Ph.D.

Divine messengers from outside your known creation dare to venture into your dream world in the effort to help you become aware of your plight. They know that the world they have entered is an illusion, which doesn't make it any easier to watch as humanity continues to brutalize, conquer and destroy each other. They ask your soul to wake up for its own sake. They feed your soul as much of the truth as your soul is prepared to absorb at any one time. They will continue until your soul — and the souls of humankind — make the choice for higher levels of awareness; for peace and love; and for knowledge and wisdom.

These divine messengers help us (including you!) transform into higher-frequency beings in order to bring new levels of awareness to the evolving soul. Luckily, when this whole insane idea was first conceived, the soul left itself an out, a very small loophole that would eventually bring humanity full circle. Imagine if the soul had made the choice to come back over and over again. This would give you the opportunity to connect with these divine messengers in many different ways and evolve gradually, waking up gently from the confusion of the illusion.

This is the evolution of the soul. Sudden awakening can be

extremely traumatic, just as being shaken out of a deep sleep can be highly disorienting. But don't worry. Becoming the best version of you is an ongoing process, not an instantaneous attainment. It is about continually becoming the best version of you in every moment.

The landscape of your dream world changes profoundly as the soul develops the ability to better see and feel reality through these healthy, wholesome, higher levels of awareness. Join us in doing what it takes to dissolve the obstacles for making the choice for a PLATINUM state of mind an automatic one.

After 25 years of rigorous scientific study, the late Dr. Valerie Hunt was internationally recognized for her pioneering research into human energy fields and consciousness. To paraphrase her, when you repress your emotion, your body hurts; when you repress your consciousness, your mind aches; when you repress your spirituality, your soul suffers.

Dr. Hunt was a high-vibrational soul who merged science and mysticism. Her impressive body of work helps the soul reset its ability to choose to journey out of the darkness, and into the Divine energy field of love. These changes are potentially irresistible to humanity's addictive nature. As your learning progresses, your spiritual development enhances your ability to discern the truth. It leads to more success in life, as well as the experience of the ineffable high of pure love. As you become a spirit junkie, your soul begins to appreciate just how crucial it is to train your ego mind.

It is a momentous time in the history of the ego mind code. The soul is shifting to timeless life codes to live by: codes whose Master Password is deliberately unprotected against theft. Steal to your heart's content, beloved. Heal your wandering soul and crippled heart. Do whatever it takes to undo the primacy of the primitive mind. Become addicted to the bliss of the dance of love and joy, as you surrender your choices to the mind of the Divine.

"If you do not change direction, you may end up where you're heading."

- Lao Tzu

Both mystics and great scientists alike have said that their experiences and experiments are guided by mystical and intuitive insight, i.e., higher awareness, which is the mind of the Divine. As astrophysicist Walter Lewin said, *"When you've discovered the truth in science, it does have the most extraordinary magical quality about it."*

When I was conversing with divine beings as a three-year-old and became convinced it was my destiny and purpose to work for God, it did not seem magical at all. It was the most normal, natural state of being I could imagine. I was aware it was a serious matter, as serious as only a three-year-old could be. I was calm, and as I accepted these revelations, somehow I knew not to talk about them to anyone — other than my mother. The look on her face when her not-quite four-year-old declared she was going to be a priest was priceless.

She told me that would not be possible because only Catholic men could be priests and we were not Catholic. I didn't know what Catholic was, but I knew I wasn't a man. Not to be deterred, the next day her little girl told her she would be a nun — they were women, right? Again she said no and explained, "If you become a nun, you will never be able to marry and have children."

In total exasperation, I put my hands on my hips and looked

her in the eye, daring her to tell me "no" again, and said, "Don't worry, Mummy; when I grow up, I will work for God. I will be a teacher and tell people the truth about love."

What the three- and four-year-old knew, I had to relearn as an adult. The spiritual world unfolded around me like a hurricane. It drew me into its orbit, sometimes tossing me around like a rag doll until I could find my way back into the calm of my PLATINUM state of mind. There have been many miraculous and extraordinary magical times since then, just as there have been many frightening ones. Through it all, I seldom lost sight of the big picture, and since her passing in 1972, my mother would drop in from her evolving life in spirit on many occasions to help me. There have been countless times, in fact, that mum has given me invaluable guidance.

SHAKE, RATTLE AND ROLL

*"Transformation literally means
going beyond your form."*

– Dr. Wayne Dyer

The Brisbane MindBodySpirit Festival, held in the huge Brisbane Convention Centre, was the venue for another massive upgrade in my awareness. I was a keynote speaker, and I also shared a small stand with a fellow healer. Thousands came daily to partake of free talks, massage, and hundreds of stands where they were offered a wide range of products and services. The colorful, bazaar-like atmosphere was like a veritable organic farmers market for the soul.

I was given fair warning the day before. The organizers of the festival requested a 'meeting' with the Divine beings I work with. At the meeting, to my surprise and chagrin, these energies I had worked with all my life thanked the organizers for the work they were doing, and explained that they were going to leverage the energy field generated by this gathering to make changes in my consciousness which would then be reflected in my body and brain function. Uh oh! I had heard this before. I was sure I would be flung back into the raging storm, but I had no idea how powerful this hurricane was destined to be.

At first, everything seemed normal. I gave people attunements of healing energy throughout the morning, as usual. My first talk at 11:00 am was well received. Afterward, on my way back to the stand, every cell in my body started shaking. My body had never done well on caffeine — one cup and I would spend the whole day on the ceiling. (If you want the cleanest house on the block, just give me a cup of coffee and a blue microfiber cleaning cloth!)

The body was reacting as though it had just absorbed 10 cups of coffee all at once. My brain began to pulse with heat and pain. It felt as though the beating of my heart had also kicked in to this symphony of shake, rattle, and roll. I was used to having to roll with the punches, but this felt like a veritable one-punch knockout.

All night and the next day, the transformational process maintained its relentless pace. I realized that the high frequency at which I was vibrating was well beyond my normal range. In addition, everyone near me was also being catalyzed in some way.

People were drawn to the energy. The line of people coming to my stand for healing grew longer. When I put my hands on one woman's head, she almost fainted. Finally able to speak, she said she felt so much better. She explained that she had been overwhelmed by white light, and the presence of a love so strong that it made her as high as a kite.

A small child who obviously had a mind of her own jumped into the chair. She had a serious expression on her beautiful face, and the dark circles under her eyes were the only other indication of anything wrong with her. When I started to give her healing her father, who was hovering over us, felt something unusual. Concerned, he cried out, "What are you doing to my daughter?"

"Don't worry, Daddy; it's heavenly," the child said. In a dreamy voice and with a huge smile on her face, she added, "I feel better now."

The day before, I had tried to greet the people in the stand opposite ours. Except for a condescending nod, they were quite unresponsive. They had taken four stands in a row, displaying huge, beautiful posters of everything Egyptian on their walls. By the third day, this spiritual storm had taken its toll on my nervous system. In almost unbearable pain, my body and brain were still shaking. One by one, the people from the everything-Egyptian stand came to our little stand with dumbstruck looks on their faces. They were not able to communicate what they were going through while this high-frequency energy field was affecting them. All they could do was stand there and stare. It was disconcerting, to say the least.

Their leader came over to me, dropped to her knees, sobbed, and held me tight. I asked her to breathe deeply and tell me what she was experiencing. She explained that at first, every time I walked past their stand, they would have flashbacks to their past lives in Egypt. By the third day, the energy field had become so powerful that it was catalyzing a constant flow of past-life recall for all of them. She said that everything started to make sense in a way they had never thought possible, and that it was a profoundly important experience for them. Now they understood why they were doing what they were doing. They had received insight into how they could change their lives, and become more successful, joyful, and loving.

Walking to the bathroom took me past the coffee stand where, long before I reached him, the man pulling coffees looked up and made a cross with his fingers to ward me off. He was there to sell coffee, and he had not put in for any changes to his consciousness. His brain was reacting to my frequency; he was feeling high and unable to focus. In sympathy, I found another route to the bathroom after that.

People's ability to experience a wider range of altered states and higher awareness increased. I was stunned when, as I walked past one stand, a complete stranger ran out to give me a gift. I knew I needed help. Another keynote speaker was on the board of the International Association of Medical Intuitives, whose members included Carolyn Myss. She was working at the stand of a good friend, and that's where I headed — with SOS written all over me.

I told my friend I needed help. She took me to the private area for participants and speakers, where we sat and waited for the medical intuitive to finish her second talk. When she arrived at our table, she took the seat furthest from me, explaining that she could not sit next to me as the energy was so strong it was knocking her around. And she had only just arrived! I didn't need to explain a thing to her. She was a highly aware person, and she was able to see, feel, and understand what was going on.

She explained that I was experiencing an overall upgrade of my being, including my brain. The process was fast-tracking the evolution of my soul, and of my brain's capacity to keep up. It was a significant transformation that enhanced my ability to tap into the human mind field and access information and light. This enabled me to better facilitate other people's transformation into higher levels of awareness. She then added that the recalibration was almost complete.

We dissected what had been happening, and we worked through the tail end of the process together. After half an hour everything seemed to be settling. The heat was dissipating, and the constant vibrations were now manageable.

As we were leaving the room, a man with a video camera on his shoulder walked past us. He had also been affected by the intensity of the energy, so he introduced himself and gave me the opening to tell him what I had seen.

I told him I could see a three-inch gray energy field around him that was not his aura. I suggested he be careful about what he ate, as he could easily put on a great deal of weight. He looked shocked and said, "But that's the weight I've just lost. I was three inches larger all over." I was seeing the energy field where he was still energetically carrying all the fat he had just lost from his physical body. This was a new trick!

The next day it was his turn to shock me. He sought me out to tell me that a woman had come to him in his dreams with a message for me. He said her name was unusual, something he had not heard before. It wasn't Ellis or Ellen but something like that. I asked him if it could have been Elva. "Yes. That was it." My mother — Elva — had chosen him to deliver a message to her daughter in distress. He told me that she had said, "Listen to the little girl." That was it.

I wanted more, but I still felt reassured that I was being looked after when I most needed it. She was reminding me of the time when her little girl had made her pronouncements about being here to work for God. If this is what it was going to take, then I just had to ride it out. The calm of the Divine Mind was only a breath away. That SOS I was wearing had broadcast out into the universe, and it brought me the best help I could have wished for.

On the last day of the festival, my new friend, the medical intuitive, asked me to help her with a young boy who was having inexplicable mystical experiences. His father had brought him to the festival every day in the hope that he would be able to understand what was happening to his son. As we walked into the stand, the young boy took one look at me and started to cry with deep, racking sobs. Instantly protective, his father stood in front of his son and asked me to leave. Both the boy and my friend cried out in unison, "No, don't go!" She asked the father to let me stay until the boy could tell us what had just happened.

Finally able to talk, he said, "I know you." With that, the boy left his seat to come and put his arms around me. With big tears still in his eyes and with so much love, he looked up at me and said, "You took me into your fashion shop and gave me a turquoise necklace you had brought from Egypt." (At twenty I had opened my first boutique. That was still my day job, which he could not have known.) "I remember you, you were my mother and the leader of our tribe. You took me to the top of the highest mountain and asked me to trust you, then you pushed me off." I asked him what happened next. He said, "I knew you would keep me safe. I just hovered there."

I was able to shed light on his experiences, and both he and his father went away calm and happy. There is a lot more to this story that might be told at another time. Suffice it to say, we all shared a happy ending.

It sounds like a fantasy; or, as many scientists have said of their discoveries, something quite magical had just happened on a mystical level. Since that experience, Daniel and I have worked with a Sydney neuroscientist who studies brainwave behavior. He hooked me up to an EEG machine while we completed some experiments, which involved attunements of this amped-up energy field without physical contact. When he tested me, my brain showed total coherence from front to back and side to side. He was stunned, and said it was most extraordinary to see a brain operating this way.

The university students who had agreed to participate in these experiments and receive this energy from us all had exams that afternoon. They unanimously reported back that they had achieved their best results in their academic careers — ever!

As you move into higher levels of awareness, you open the door to whole new worlds — worlds where anything is possible. It is as simple and straightforward as training your ego mind to get out of the way, so that the Divine Mind can reveal its wondrous mysteries.

Courageously make the decision to move beyond your physical form and senses, and focus on the divine gifts you have been given to share with the world. Become your own hero. Experience the magical states of your mystical being.

"Changing is not just changing the things outside of us. First of all we need the right view that transcends all notions of being and non-being, creator and creature, mind and spirit. That kind of insight is crucial for transformation and healing."

— *Thich Nhat Hanh*

BRAINS WIRED DIFFERENTLY

A woman who was doing her university thesis on channeling asked to sit in on one of my presentations. During the evening I invited questions. With determination, her hand shot up first. She smugly said, "Scientists in England believe that people like you who think they can channel just have their brains wired differently from the rest of us. What do you think about that?" With a calm I was not feeling, the Divine energy working with me at that moment gently looked into her eyes and with all the love in the world said, "Oh, that the rest of the world had their brains wired like this!"

I knew that beyond simply channeling, my mind was working with a strong connection to the Divine Mind. The higher frequencies used when I am connecting in this way overlap with the unusual (but more limited) frequency range that typically shows up when people channel. This is a classic example of Valerie Hunt's description of higher vibrational states, in which one experiences transcendental ideas and shares insights about ultimate sources of reality.

The divine beings I had worked with all my life had filled the room with their high vibrations. People described what they were feeling. Without exception, they reported being enveloped in the presence of a love so profound they felt they could touch it — yes, even the woman writing her thesis. Even though they could not remember all the words, they had nonetheless been transported into their hearts. The mind field, or we could also say the heart field, was palpable, lingering in the room well after the session was over.

As is typical when working with us, people had moved into a high vibrational state that is classically associated with enlightenment. No one wanted to leave the love, and the safe haven, that had been energetically created that night.

"Where there is great love

there are always

miracles."

– Willa Cather

GOOD VODKA AND ROTTEN MEAT

When you operate in codes made by lower-consciousness programmers you produce a symphony that features a duet of death and destruction. Like a computer that only functions according to the codes of its programs, your body and reptilian brain are simply storage and processing units for your conscious and unconscious thoughts, ideas, and beliefs — your programs.

To illustrate how important the consciousness of the programmer is in your lives, I like to share this story. Some of the earliest computers were given the job of translating a simple phrase from English to Russian and back again. The phrase was, "The spirit is willing, but the flesh is weak." The resulting phrase came back as, "The vodka is good, but the meat is rotten."

Your amazing human computer functions by its many codes. Anyone who is aware of the passwords can operate by their code of choice rather than by default. Every response is determined by the code that is operating. Each 'topic file, such as 'mother' or 'brother,' contains all the information you have unconsciously stored about that person or topic. How you understand, interpret, and respond to that information depends upon which code is in use.

You have to use a password to activate a code before it is ready to launch, but what code are you launching? Is the meat rotten, the spirit willing, the vodka good, or the flesh weak? Do not assume we have all programmed in the same codes, and that we should understand each other easily. When the codes are different, meaning and mutual understanding get lost in translation.

This is the equivalent of the files that the ego mind has programmed and stored in the conscious and unconscious mind. Using your passwords launches the programs, whether good or bad, into the processing unit for the whole world to see. Like any computer, your biological human computer is full of glitches, bugs, cookies and spam, viruses, and compromised codes that vary depending on the programmers who have had access. This includes your parents, siblings, children, teachers, friends, and lovers, not to mention media, Internet, movies, music, games, and everything else the human mind creates.

If you ignore signs such as negativity, fear, and pain, like any computer you may crash, get sick, and even die. When this happens to your electronic device, you trade it in for a newer, better model. In the case of your human computer, when you die you come back in a new model, ever hopeful that it will function better than the last one.

Although enriched by the experiences of all your lifetimes, this new model still gets created with the same life codes as the last one.

It is always your soul's choice which code to use. Ultimately, there are only two choices.

Just as the evolution of your soul proceeds at an open-ended pace, by accessing higher levels of awareness you can revise your codes to continually upgrade to a more vital and happier life.

You need to be operating in the Divine Mind code to identify the faulty program and discover its cause. Only then can you neutralize the program and delete the effect of past events that sabotage you. This automatically raises your awareness.

Diligently seek the truth. Get neutral, forgive, and be happy.

Unlike in arithmetic, being 'right' in relationships is a matter of interpretation. In life, being 'right' is a matter of context and meaning, and it depends on the code you are operating in. When your ego mind programs get triggered, consider asking yourself, "Would I rather be happy or be right?"

"Most folks are as happy as

they make up

their minds to be."

– Abraham Lincoln

WHO'S PROGRAMMING YOU?

The most obvious programmers are your parents. Parental love, especially your mother's, is a critical factor in conditioning the limbic brain to facilitate making healthy, emotionally strong, and loving decisions as you get older. The presence of your loving father, extended family, and community also play an integral role in your becoming socially balanced and well adjusted.

The mind field you grow up in affects you on every level, and it either supports your growth or suppresses it. Your life codes and passwords are a work in progress. You can choose ego mind codes and make it hard work, or Divine Mind codes and have lots more fun and success.

If you've chosen to have more fun, diligently use the Divine Mind Code's Master Password to create new habit fields. As you do, you will rewire your brain, which further ensures the success of the reprogramming process into higher awareness.

With your higher awareness, and by using the Master Password to make the Divine Mind Code your default operating code, you have thus assured your PLATINUM life.

Dr. Hunt explains that when a person's mind field reached higher levels of awareness, which corresponds to higher vibrational states, they experienced *"knowing, higher information, transcendental ideas, insight about ultimate sources of reality, and creativity in its pure form. Thoughts were grander, more penetrating, and global."*

YOU ARE WHAT YOU THINK

"One of the biggest insights of cognitive neuroscience is that we see the world as we construct it - not as it is."

- Donald Hoffman, Ph.D., Professor, Dept. of Cognitive Sciences. University of California, Irvine

The physical body responds either positively or negatively not only to what you say and do, but also to what you think. The good news is that it responds to what you think consciously. The bad news is that it is always responding to what you think unconsciously. In Bruce Lipton's book *The Biology of Belief,* he observes that the subconscious mind processes 20 million environmental stimuli per second, versus 40 environmental stimuli by the conscious mind in the same second. Thus, the information-processing capacity of the unconscious mind is 500,000 times greater than the conscious mind. Can you guess which one prevails whenever there is a conflict?

Your latest tweet, Facebook feed, or news flash will always be good or bad depending on your level of awareness in the moment.

Your health, happiness, and level of success depend on how you use awareness to deal with conflict.

If you are still operating in caveman consciousness (below 200 x 200 on the Integrated Wholeness Scale), your unaware mind and primitive brain would tend to deal with conflict by trampling all over everyone, plotting revenge, and sometimes even killing just because someone has looked at you the wrong way. True forgiveness depends upon unconditional love, which starts at 540 x 540 on the Integrated Wholeness Scale. It is obviously foreign to this primitive state of awareness.

As humans evolve toward enlightenment, scientists have discovered there are emotional, mental, and even physical needs for forgiveness. Every cell in your body acts like a computer. They have an electromagnetic energy field and a biochemical composition that instantly responds to your environment — and to your thoughts about it.

More than anything else, the body's response to your conscious and unconscious thoughts determines whether you have good health or disease.

Genetic inheritance is only a predisposition, according to the latest discoveries in epigenetics. Whether it is triggered or not is most often dependent on the individual. The totality of your beliefs, ideas, and programs determines, for example, whether you will forgive or not. This in turn stimulates your happy or unhappy hormonal responses — and hence your happy or unhappy experience of life.

Redefining and using forgiveness is critically important to your overall quality of life, health, and happiness.

"Holding on to anger is just like grasping a hot coal with the intent of throwing it at someone else; you are the one who gets burned."

– Buddha

"Holding a grudge can kill you," says Jay D. Roberts, MD, after a Harvard Medical study discovered that unforgiveness can cause many symptoms and diseases, including:

Inflammation

Increased cortisol

Auto-immune problems

Heart disease and cancer

Severe headaches

Stomach and abdominal problems

Increased stress

Insomnia

The study goes on to show 5 major benefits of forgiveness:

Reduced stress

Better heart health

Stronger relationships

Reduced pain

Greater happiness

Your choice of code determines your thoughts — and your thoughts determine your life.

Where you are in the evolution of your soul determines your choice of passwords that access either corrupted or inspirational encoding. Your life becomes happier, healthier, and richer as your soul chooses the Divine Mind Code. You develop gratitude, kindness, generosity, compassion, and the ability to love unconditionally and truly forgive. Your body, mind, and soul become stronger, more vital, and more attractive.

Only your awakened soul can make the conscious choice to bring in the Divine Mind as its new programmer. Take the time and use the Quantum Neutrality process to neutralize the programs developed in the ego mind's world — and then delete their effects. Choose to forgive the painful results of those programs. If left unforgiven, they would only continue to corrupt your system and sabotage your life with devastating results.

Inquiring deeply into your conscious and unconscious

programs, and getting to the core beliefs around any feelings of fear, negativity, and pain, is the best way to avoid illness. This will turbocharge your evolutionary expedition into wholeness. The more whole you become, the less space there is for the ego mind to buck at having its stories undone — and at having to forgive — even if it is in enlightened self-interest.

"Reality is neither fact nor fiction but is the emphasis we place on various parts of our stream of consciousness...

that consciousness is a continuum extending from material awareness to higher awareness. The mind experiences by means of its awareness."

– Valerie V. Hunt, Ph.D.

INDIANA JONES AND THE TOWN OF FORGIVENESS

In search of the grand prize of immortal life and everlasting love, imagine you have become an archeologist. Passionate about digging around in the ancient grounds of your split mind, you are excited to find even the smallest sliver of evidence that will give your life genuine meaning and fulfillment. Combing through the archives of the split mind reveals the need to be gentle with yourself. Rather than jump all over this ancient site like a bulldozer, you need to research it well, treading carefully among the ruins of your life to learn where you came from, and where it is possible for you to go.

That does not mean pussyfooting around, though. Like Indiana Jones in the movie *The Temple of Doom*, your ventures into the Temple of the Divine Mind have thrown you many curve balls. Often you feel like running for your life, with huge boulders and oversized spiders of your imagination out to get you.

That all stops when you resolve the past emotions and subsequent decisions you made not to go into this mystical world, which you thought was full of danger. You have made innumerable attempts at finding this precious jewel of brilliant light, in other temples and in so many other lifetimes, and often with devastating results.

In some, where you did discover the Mind of the Divine, you were almost always used and abused for having 'supernatural' power. In others, you were burned at the stake, drowned, or crucified — or you literally lost your head. Your presence as a healer or enlightened being could not be tolerated by the then-prevailing culture, power structure, or religious establishment. That kind of overwhelming emotional upheaval sent you spinning into disbelief and confusion — and instantly reverting to the ego mind code.

The ego mind delights in subverting your adventure. It exploits your anger for its own purposes, turning you against the God who appeared not to save you when your cries for help went unheard. As Dr. Hunt says, "Our miscast anger at God has denied us access to our divine power ... without guilt, we can see how our humanness [i.e., the ego mind] has played such a devastating trick on us."

In the heat of emotional trauma, you reacted to these events by making decisions such as: 'Being spiritual is dangerous; I must hide my light and connection to the Divine.' 'I have to keep my head down and not stand out. It's not safe to be different, to be powerful, to be a healer.' And naturally, 'If God even exists, He certainly doesn't love or care about me.'

These became the programs stored deep in the unconscious mind. The Divine Mind's natural magnetic pull to the soul never wavers. However, per its habit, the unevolved soul allows the ego mind to jump in to activate the 'savior' code at any opportunity. Ego mind does not want you on any more adventures into the mystical realms of the exotic territory of your heart. It will tirelessly do whatever it can to subvert the magnetic pull of the Divine Mind to your heart — which it perceives as a threat.

The ego mind has conned the frightened soul into becoming complicit in making the choice to hide and lock away the mystical world of your spirituality.

But your natural state of being cannot be held hostage forever: it only feels that way. Your treasure map has led you to a place and time on the evolutionary journey of your soul where all these ancient, illusory ideas are losing their ability to distract you from your destination.

You are asking important questions like: Who am I? Why am I here? Where does the power of the human mind reside? How do I decode my own life, let alone those of the rest of the world? The answers are found by exploring an ancient but well-hidden location. You have finally deciphered the Master Password PLATINUM — the password that leads you to the only real destination to be found on this heavily encoded map. The place marked X is in the town of Forgiveness, right in the center of the state of Unconditional Love.

The light and love you have been seeking has always been right inside your sleeping mind.

Your archeological dig has gone deep enough into your limited world of misperceptions, judgments, and projections to discover that the real power of the human mind does not live inside the dream. In this enlightening age of quantum physics, scientists have finally discovered what mystics have known for millennia: the holographic mind of man — the microcosm — and the entire holistic cosmos — the macrocosm — are inextricably interconnected, and they are interacting constantly.

The real answers come from the mystical realms of the intuitive heart, which can instantly teleport you to the town of Forgiveness in your mind.

With the use of heightened awareness guided by clear intention, you can use intuition and the power of forgiveness to instantly correct misperceptions, delete the effects of emotional baggage, and bring about peace in minutes.

The decoding process happens more efficiently as you get clearer and clearer with the release of your outdated ideas and corrupted programs. It is as though your life has been built on smoke and mirrors by the best FX people in the world. Stepping out of the 3D sci-fi horror movie of guilt, shame, and blame; separation and intolerance; ignorance, lies, and pain is as easy as leaving this illusory movie set and finally going home for the day. Home is in the heart of your True Self.

Nothing — wrong turns, road blocks, detours, faulty GPS systems, even getting lost for what seems like lifetimes — deters aware, high-frequency beings from their mission to find their way back to the safe haven of the Divine Mind.

Encode your GPS system for destination Forgiveness, that town in the heart of the real world — and don't stop driving until you get there. Be not deceived by ego mind's illusory town of the same name, which is just another name for judgment.

Recalculating the course to Forgiveness, even after ending up in the town of Judgment, automatically corrects perceptions. From the magnetic, lofty peaks of Forgiveness, your heart knows no boundaries. No longer limited by the maze of the place you came from, as you forgive from that higher perspective, you experience profound relief and exhilarating freedom — and you become aware that you yourself are forgiven, too.

EGO PUPPY TRAINING #3: AWARENESS

If you have not yet read *PEACE: Power Up Your Life* and *LOVE: Ignite The Secret To Your Success*, the first two books in The CODEBREAKER PLATINUM Series, you probably don't know that at birth you acquired an Ego Puppy and a Karma Kitten. It is your job to train your Ego Puppy, which in 'reality' is your ego mind. Your Karma Kitten is your connection to your intuition and the Divine within you. Cultivating your relationship with her enhances your higher awareness.

Although at first Karma Kittens only use their physical eyes, they quickly develop vision via their spiritual eyes: seeing, feeling, and intuiting the real world via the Divine Mind Code.

They are an important aspect of your being, which your soul uses to get back into your heart. They can also exert a constructive impact on those Ego Puppies who are being trained to fulfill their destiny to live a life of meaning and purpose. "Once well trained, like great service dogs, they dedicate their lives just like police dogs, guide dogs, farm dogs, and all manner of loyal and loving companions."

They too are love junkies who seek constant reassurance that they are okay, and that it's all good.

Have you ever noticed how a puppy will keep coming back for more love, play, and attention even after you have scolded it? Puppies easily surrender resentment at being disciplined. Aware Ego Puppies do not even consider the need to forgive; in a nanosecond they are on to the next adventure.

The training process always involves stress for both Ego Puppy and those who commit to train them. Remember, this is your ego mind we are talking about, so ultimately your only choice is when you will do it.

Train your Ego Puppy with love, and be firm about the choices that must be made. Help it come into higher levels of awareness. No piddling all over anyone else, no pooping inside, no scaring small children or growling at postmen, and definitely no biting. Little Ego's training depends on you.

Your soul chooses the codes you live by. It can choose the Divine Mind Code, in which you will love, train, and teach Ego Puppy how to have the life of their puppy dreams as a beloved member of their new family. Alternatively, the soul can default to the ego mind code, which will create a dangerous monster who thinks he or she has no choice but to fight just to survive. Don't let your Ego Puppy turn into a primitive alpha canine — or even worse, a junkyard dog.

Wherever you go is where Ego Puppy is. Undo the damage that past training and conditioning have wrought, and bring your Ego Puppy back to love. Let your intuitive Karma Kitten loose. Let them play, and watch as Ego Puppy falls in love in an unlikely partnership.

"Mind mastery is the soul's

unavoidable journey."

— Valerie V. Hunt, Ph.D.

"Intuition will tell the thinking mind

where to look next...

I work with it and rely on it.

It's my partner."

— *Jonas Salk, M.D.*
Discoverer of the first polio vaccine

JUMP-START THE PROCESS

"Man is a credulous animal and must believe something. In the absence of good grounds for belief, he will be satisfied with bad ones."

– Bertrand Russell

The CODEBREAKER PLATINUM Series presents a systematic process that you can adapt to suit your own needs and lifestyle to power up your life, ignite your secret to success, and discover how life really works. It contains a wide range of simple tools, techniques, and practices that all complement and reinforce one another. They fall into the two categories that encompass all fundamental approaches to inner development in every spiritual and personal development tradition: inquiry and attunement.

INQUIRY practices are those in which you ask yourself questions.

ATTUNEMENT practices are those in which you harmonize your own frequency with a frequency of your choice.

INQUIRY: To begin, we present these simple but powerful inquiry techniques: The Four Questions, True Self Reprogramming, Rate Your State, and the Quantum Neutrality Process. Empowered neutrality is where you consistently correct emotional blocks that stop you from living the best version of you. To get you started, we have outlined the first simple steps so that you can correct emotional blocks and go from feeling awful to feeling awesome in minutes.

ATTUNEMENT: Reading this series of books attunes you to the enlightenment frequency, as does working with us at our live events and in our virtual and digital programs. Another attunement practice we strongly recommend is meditation. We offer you a link to a free guided meditation on our website (www.TheBiskinds.com) which you are welcome to download and use as often as you can. We suggest using it at least once daily.

The more you use these tools, the more you will get from them. Not only will you become more skillful in their use, but their impact is cumulative.

This is an introduction to a lifelong system that can take you as far and as high on the Map of Awareness and the Integrated Wholeness Scale as you are prepared to go. Have fun! And remember, your thoughts are the only thing stopping you from having the life you want.

A MEDITATION ON AWARENESS

Begin by observing your breath and letting your body relax. As you allow your thoughts to simply come and go, release all judgments. Center yourself by taking a few deep breaths, and align yourself to a place of peace.

Continue to breathe comfortably, and think of someone or something you love. Feel your whole being make the shift to the powerful vibrational frequency of the love that you are. As you fully connect to your True Self, you easily access your intuition and higher awareness. In this moment, you have transcended your ego mind programs. Fear, pride, worry, guilt, shame, and blame have been replaced by love.

Now imagine, see, or feel a column of white light pouring into the top of your head and filling your body, right down to your feet and toes. This is the light of your True Self, and of its attribute: higher awareness. Allow this white light to flow freely, getting hotter and stronger as you stay aware of your breath, your body relaxing even more. You can do this! If you are having trouble imagining this white light, know that it is still there whether you are aware of it or not. Just the act of thinking about it invites it to work its magic in your life.

Share your intention for your soul to continually choose the code that facilitates this connection with your True Self. Let my words be your words: *"I choose to live from this place of love and higher awareness, fully aligned to my True Self."*

Bask in the feeling of being this love. It has no conditions. There is nothing you need to do, give, or get. The Divine Mind has taken center stage, and you are the star in the middle of this amazing show.

With every breath you take, your body, mind, and soul are

being regenerated, rejuvenated, strengthened, and renewed. You know, with every fiber of your being, that the love that you are is your pathway to success. You have discovered how life really works, and you have ignited the secret to better relationships.

You have more vitality, and expanded creativity, and the ability to direct your soul to choose to stay in this place of trust, presence, and strength — to live in the real world of the Divine. Know that you and the stars are all made of the same stuff. There is only one spirit filling seven billion different beings, and you are aware of the Divinity within each of their True Selves.

Stay in this expanded place, basking in the peace, love, and awareness that you are, for as long as you can. Totally aligned with this unfathomably rich place of union with your intuition, expanded awareness, and love, you naturally experience the oneness of all life.

You are now in tune with the frequency of higher awareness and the vibration of love. This meditation powerfully activates the best version of you. Share it with the world. Make it your intention to use your full expression of love, and your gift of higher awareness, to stay on this frequency for as long as you can.

Recall this experience any time you feel yourself slipping into fear, negativity, or pain. Use it to realign with your True Self by imagining this white light and your superconscious state of oneness with all life. With awareness, ignite the high frequency of love as you sense yourself fully connected to the Divine within you — as you.

When you are ready, take a few more deep breaths, gently stretch out your body, and slowly open your eyes.

THE FOUR QUESTIONS: AWARENESS

This inquiry technique makes full use of your internal GPS.

It is based on the use of mindfulness, which is simply observing yourself without judgment. It is intentional self-awareness. This simple but powerful tool cultivates your emotional intelligence.

Your feelings are your readout on your internal GPS. The more negative you are feeling, the more off course you are. The better you feel, the more on course you are. Making repeated course corrections is an easy, effective, and reliable way to change your state.

Make a habit of checking in with this internal GPS to connect with your true north, your True Self.

Use this simple set of questions to change the way you feel from one moment to the next. As you practice and become proficient, this technique will become second nature — and you will use it like an aircraft's autopilot to course-correct automatically, back to your natural state of peace and love.

Use the Four Questions whenever you feel out of control, when the ego mind has you out of balance, and any time you feel you have moved away from your natural state of awareness. Recognize that it is only the untrained ego mind doing its thing. Answer the questions truthfully and spontaneously. Keep focused on the answer to question number four as long as you can.

This is an example only. Use your own words and the wisdom of your own heart to answer these questions.

1. What am I Feeling?

Unsettled.

2. What am I Focused on?

Nothing is ever good enough.

3. How do I want to Feel?

I want to feel clear and certain.

4. What Focus will serve that?

My True Self always provides guidance I can trust.

Be grateful for your all-knowing intuition, and be aware that when someone hurts you, or you hurt yourself, it is only ever a cry for love. Use your higher awareness to discover how you can help others who are in need. Tell your ego mind to sit and stay, while you plunge into your heart and go straight for the treasure marked with an X in the town of Forgiveness.

RATE YOUR STATE: AWARENESS

Use these questions to guide you into attaining higher levels of awareness on the Integrated Wholeness Scale. Depending on the answers at any given time, you just might need to change your codes.

1. When you walk into a room, a street, or a neighborhood, are you aware of the energy field that is prevalent at that time? Do you feel safe or unsafe?

You have the power to discern whether you should stay or leave a place depending on your GPS alerts. Your body will give you clues by feeling uncomfortable or not. Tapping into the virtual omniscience of your higher awareness has you rising high and fast on the Integrated Wholeness Scale.

2. Are you aware of how your words and actions affect those around you?

The most successful leaders, entrepreneurs, executives, and companies become and remain aware of the happiness of the people around them. You are high on the Integrated Wholeness Scale when you use your awareness to discern what needs to be said and done for the highest and best for all concerned.

3. How much effort are you prepared to put into training yourself to get neutral and forgive? How much are you investing in yourself to get neutral and succeed in love and life?

Becoming aware of how your ego mind programs affect others is of paramount importance for being able to change your language and behavior in order to have the relationships and success you deserve. Stay high, at the level of love or above on the Integrated Wholeness Scale, and access your True Self where real forgiveness, courage, acceptance, and tolerance bring you back into your heart, into love, and into heightened states of awareness.

Your new life codes cultivate your noble purpose in becoming an aware, enlightened presence on this planet: to love unconditionally, even through adversity, and to internalize the Master Password PLATINUM to facilitate becoming whole. In this state, which is your destiny, you are an amazing gift to the world.

TRUE SELF REPROGRAMMING

Whenever you are feeling fear, negativity, shame, blame, guilt, or pain, ask yourself, "When did I start to feel like this?"

Track your thoughts back to the source. It might not necessarily have been a major challenge; it could have been something quite innocent that triggered an ego mind program that set off your emotional response.

For example, your partner might have looked at you in a way you perceived as disapproving. At lightning speed, the ego mind triggers programs like, "I'm not good enough. What's wrong with me?" And at the same speed, you have moved away from your perfect point of power, which is the frequency of love and success.

Once you have pinpointed the program, you can neutralize it and delete its effects by using The Quantum Neutrality Process.

You can also use True Self Reprogramming.

1. Clear yourself by thumping your thymus. Think of someone or something you love, and maintain that feeling. Smile!

2. Having identified the offending program (e.g., "I don't get it. I never get it. I never know the answer"), look into your eyes in a mirror, and from your heart, with the feeling of unconditional love, say, "I am in perfect harmony with my True Self. With higher awareness, I always bring the best version of myself to every situation. My higher awareness provides perfect wisdom, insight, and guidance for every situation, for the highest and best for all concerned."

3. Create new neural pathways by repeating these positive attributes for one minute every few hours for one month.

This process works to balance your whole being — mentally, emotionally, physically, spiritually, and psychologically. Whatever challenge you may face, and even if you have lost belief in yourself, the True Self Reprogramming statements are a powerful reminder of your true essence: "My True Self is perfect. I am worthy of success and love. I am in harmony with my True Self, and I always bring the best version of myself to every situation. I resonate with the energy frequency of love. My higher awareness provides perfect wisdom, insight, and guidance for every situation, for the highest and best for all concerned."

THE ULTIMATE MIND SHIFT: AN INTRODUCTION TO QUANTUM NEUTRALITY — THE FIRST STEPS

It's time to put your discovery of how life really works into action.

The Quantum Neutrality Process is the art and science of identifying and neutralizing your blocks — and deleting their effects. As you make the ultimate mind shift, you heighten your awareness, access your personal power, and make better decisions about life, love, and relationships. This restores strength and energy to your body, mind, and soul.

1. Your information center is composed of your midline, core, and spine, and your central and peripheral nervous systems. You can correct and strengthen the components of your information center by closing your eyes and imagining more of your True Self, in the form of white light, pouring in through the top of your head and filling your whole being.

If you are not seeing or feeling the light, don't quit. Keep going until you do; simply use your imagination. If you are still not connecting to the white light, take yourself into the sunshine or sit under a hot spotlight. That's it. You can do this!

Imagining your True Self in the form of white light filling your being corrects the information center, relaxes you, and informs the ego mind that it is time to sit and stay, to listen and learn without comment.

2. Discover the issue responsible for taking you out of balance by tapping into your intuition. Intuition is a core

element of higher awareness. It is the powerhouse within your mainframe. It identifies passwords and deciphers faulty codes running in your human computer.

Your intuition accesses information from the Divine Mind field, and it quickly helps you discover where you are weak or strong. What is the answer? Concentrate. Focus. Determine to access your intuition and have it work for you.

How many times have you experienced this? Say you're doing a Google search, and after only one word, or even just a part of a word, the computer appears to read your mind — and in a flash, complete thoughts appear. Intuition works in a similar way. The Divine Mind code assembles millions of life experiences and provides you with an immediate 'Executive Summary.'

Intuition is always ready for your use. Some people call it a gut feeling or an inner knowing. The more you use it, the stronger it gets, and the more effective your corrections become. Your intuition can instantly identify what programs make you feel weak or strong, but if you do not trust it yet, use muscle testing or kinesiology to confirm the source of the weakness. We also develop this further in our programs, trainings, and live events.

When you feel discomfort — such as fear, negativity, or pain — a program has been triggered, and you need to get neutral. You might think you know what needs to be worked on, but in every case it is never what you think it is. All disease, distress, and discomfort first originate within the mind field, and only then are they felt as pain. All symptoms begin with a lack of love.

The cause is always found in an ego mind program that shows up as a belief or idea. You brought programs into this lifetime with you, as well as acquiring them from your environment. Usually, you will not identify or even relate with the original programs, as they have been buried deep in the storage section — the unconscious mind — of your computer for so long you have forgotten they were even there.

3. Apply the Quantum Neutrality Process and say, either aloud or to yourself, "I neutralize all beliefs, ideas, and patterns associated with this program on a physical, mental, emotional, psychological, psychic, and spiritual level." Your intention will determine your results. Don't just say it. Feel it. Mean it. Know — and feel — that it's done.

4. Now say aloud or to yourself, "I delete all karma and habitual thinking related to this program." Imagine and, if helpful, visualize the weight lifting off your shoulders. Know — and feel — that it's done.

5. With unconditional love, forgive everything and everyone who has hurt you, including yourself, that are associated with the program you have just corrected. Even if you need to start with just one person and a small or trivial issue, forgive everyone and everything involved.

As you follow these steps, the emotional charge around the information in the program dissolves. In fact, you will not be able to find the old emotional feelings and reactions once they have been corrected. Often you will feel a shift in your body, once the relevant mental and emotional energy has been discharged in this way.

A feeling of relief is the first sign that the program has been corrected and you are neutral to the event. You will feel empowered to move forward, free of the blocks to your inner peace. Your body, mind, and soul will now realign with your personal power, and you will be empowered to regenerate, rejuvenate, strengthen, and renew your entire energy system. If you cannot get neutral around an event or issue, consider participating in a program with us, either live or virtual, where we provide more in-depth training and we demonstrate this process by working with participants as examples.

This is an introduction to Quantum Neutrality, a groundbreaking process that is invaluable and life-changing. We treat it more fully in *NEUTRALITY: Go Beyond Positive — Your Key to Freedom*, the sixth book in The CODEBREAKER PLATINUM Series. We also address this in still more depth in our programs, trainings, and live events.

CULTIVATING AWARENESS

Nothing outside yourself can provide the insights you need in any moment the way your awareness can.

Consistently attune yourself to the frequency of success and love. Like a prayer, these statements form an energy field that you broadcast out to the cosmos while aligning you with the Divine Mind Code. By cultivating peace and love, you provide the essential ground for higher awareness to flourish.

Bring the best version of who you are into every situation. Connect fully to the higher awareness that you are, and unleash the immeasurable power of the Divine Mind. The incredible insights available to higher awareness are boundless.

Change your thoughts — higher awareness is not something you have to get, give, or do. It is who you are. Seek the highest and best for all concerned.

Change your life — higher awareness is an attribute of the awesome energy that is who you are. You are what you have been looking for, and your higher awareness shows it to you.

Change the world — use your higher awareness to help you be the transformation you want to see in the world, and the world will become a vibrational match to your inspired vision.

Intentionally be a mirror for the awareness and love that others are, especially when their programs are acting as obstacles to that greatness.

When you express the awesomeness that you are, you give others permission to do the same.

To paraphrase Michael Jackson, if you want to make the world a better place, take a look at yourself and then make the change you want to see.

A QUICK OVERVIEW: AWARENESS

"Yesterday I was clever,
so I wanted to change the world.
Today I am wise, so I am changing myself."

– Rumi

Live the successful life you deserve. Here are some key points to help you activate and access new levels of awareness.

HIGHER AWARENESS transcends the realm of the ego mind.

The ego mind code can only operate in your unconscious and conscious states. It wants to disconnect you from your True Self's higher awareness, so that you remain separate, clueless, and dependent on it.

Higher awareness automatically gets the big picture and sees the forest — not only the trees. Your imagination, creativity, and intuition thrive when your soul cultivates higher awareness, which simultaneously accesses your superconsciousness and everyday consciousness, as well as your unconscious mind.

With Divine Mind awareness, you know you are part of a unified field of information and energy. You naturally intuit the right thing to say and do, for the highest and best for all concerned.

That part of your being which is connected to the Divine Mind field has the capacity for virtual omniscience. It is capable of an infinite range of seemingly mysterious and magical feats.

But they are only mysterious to the ego mind. In the realm of the Divine Mind, access to all knowledge is available to everyone.

Higher awareness is a cornerstone to having a happy, successful, and fulfilled life.

Ego mind awareness is Newtonian, and it is totally invested in the physical world. The unconscious programs that were created during times of emotional stress will always subvert and stop your expansion into higher awareness.

Divine Mind awareness operates according to Quantum Field Theory, in which everything is interconnected. It posits that even the simple act of looking at something — not to mention *how* you look at it — changes it on an atomic and subatomic level. Let's take it one step further: the very act of thinking about someone or something changes them or it.

Knowledge is of the Divine Mind; perception is of the ego mind.

Your ego mind has created almost unbreakable codes that it has convincingly brainwashed you into thinking are necessary to keep you safe. But neither it nor its codes can do that. They are not real.

As science and technology and spirituality converge, small but growing numbers of us are beginning to decipher the timeless life codes of the Divine Mind, and move into new levels of awareness. Only there are you truly safe. Only there can you experience pure love.

You have a body whose job it is to communicate with you and the cosmos. It is always doing this, but are you always listening? Active use of your higher awareness, your sixth sense, is essential for the Divine Mind Code to be fully operational and to optimize your connection to the cosmos.

Your five senses work in conjunction with you in this wondrous film that is your life. It is inappropriate to say that it's weird when your natural ability to use your awareness gives you a gut feeling. Nor is it 'woo woo' to you use your powers of observation, discernment, and intuition to understand what needs to be said or done in any situation.

You have this ability. Your noble purpose in life includes evolving and growing your awareness so that in any given moment, your soul consistently chooses the Divine Mind code. As you do this, your life becomes the magnificent creation you've always wanted it to be.

How you use awareness to deal with conflict is critical to your health, happiness, and level of success.

The landscape of this illusory dreamworld transforms as your soul sees, feels, and develops the ability to make the choice for love, and light, and higher awareness.

Profound transformation happens when high-vibrational beings merge science and spirituality, and inspire the soul to restore its ability to choose the way out of darkness and into love. These empowering and often mystical experiences are potentially irresistible to humanity's addictive nature.

As you move into higher levels of awareness, you open the door to a whole new world — a world where anything is possible. It is as simple as training the ego mind to get out of the way, so that the Divine Mind can reveal its wondrous mysteries.

Every cell in your body acts like a computer. Their biochemical composition and electromagnetic energy fields instantly respond to your thoughts. More than anything else, the body's response to your conscious and unconscious thoughts determines whether you have good health or disease.

The totality of your beliefs, ideas, and programs determines your happy or unhappy hormonal responses, and thus your happy or unhappy experience of life.

With the use of heightened awareness guided by clear intention, you can use intuition and the power of forgiveness to instantly correct misperceptions, delete the effects of emotional baggage — and bring about peace in moments.

Where you are in the evolution of your soul influences your choice of passwords, which in turn activate corrupted or inspirational encoding. Your life becomes happier and healthier as your soul makes the choice for enlightenment. You develop gratitude, kindness, generosity, compassion, and the incomparable ability to love unconditionally and truly forgive.

The aware soul makes the conscious choice to enlist the Divine Mind as its new programmer, as it takes the time to identify and neutralize the programs and beliefs developed in the ego mind's world. It understands that left alone, they would only continue to corrupt the system.

Delving into your conscious and unconscious programs, and getting to the truth behind any feeling of fear, negativity, and pain is the ultimate way to avoid illness. Don't be afraid. This will turbocharge your evolutionary expedition into wholeness. The more whole you become, the less room there is for the ego mind to buck at having its stories unraveled.

Your soul cannot avoid making choices. Not choosing is still your choice. As the evolutionary process unfolds at its open-ended pace, you can continually choose to change your codes to reach higher levels of awareness. This supports a happy and vital life.

Diligently seek and reveal the truth. Correct your programs by dissolving the emotional charge from past events, and canceling your internal decisions that resulted from them. This is the way you can forgive, become neutral free, and; at last experience inner peace, unconditional love, and true happiness.

This is a critical time in the history of the ego mind code. The soul is shifting to timeless life codes to live by, whose Master Passwords are deliberately unprotected against theft. Steal away to your heart's content, beloved. Heal your wandering soul and crippled heart. Do whatever it takes to undo the primacy of the primitive mind.

Become addicted to the bliss of the dance of love and joy. With higher awareness, revel in your surrender of your ego mind's choices to the mind of the Divine.

Your life codes and passwords are a work in progress. Your choice will either make it hard work, or make it simple and fun. Training the mind rewires the brain by creating new neural pathways, which naturally enhances the sustainability of your reprogramming process into higher awareness.

With the use of heightened awareness guided by clear intention, you can use intuition and the power of forgiveness to instantly correct misperceptions, delete the effects of emotional baggage, and bring about peace in minutes.

The light and love you have been seeking has always been right inside your sleeping mind.

JUST A REMINDER: It's Okay. It's Not Real. It's just a story. And you can change it any time you like!

"What quantum physics teaches us is that everything we thought is physical is not physical."

— Bruce Lipton, Ph.D.

You are now ready to move on to the next keyword in the Master Password. As you move forward on life's greatest adventure, and you build upon Peace, Love, and Awareness as your foundation, we invite you to take the next step in connecting with the best version of you — Trust.

TRUST: I trust that my True Self can discern the truth in any situation -- which frees me from fear.

Trust: Cultivate True Confidence is the fourth book in The CODEBREAKER PLATINUM Series. As you Trust in the order of all things, you will strengthen your connection with your True Self with real confidence, and with the energy frequency of enlightenment.

Access the tools and resources at **www.TheBiskinds.com**. Collect all eight books in The CODEBREAKER PLATINUM Series, starting with *PEACE, LOVE, AWARENESS*, and *TRUST*.

http://thebiskinds.com/peace
http://thebiskinds.com/love
http://thebiskinds.com/awareness

PEACE: Power Up Your Life,
LOVE: Ignite the Secret to Your Success
AWARENESS: Discover How Life Really Works
TRUST: Cultivate True Confidence
INTEGRITY: Master Your Inner Strength
NEUTRALITY: Go Beyond Positive – Your Key To Freedom
UNITY: Connect The Dots To Ultimate Happiness
MINDFULNESS: Access Your Awesome Potential

We are excited to continue to work together!
With warmest love and blessings,
Sandra and Daniel

ABOUT SANDRA AND DANIEL

The Biskinds share their expertise in personal transformation as thought leaders, authors, teachers, professional speakers, and consultants. They are also coaches and mentors. Both have had highly successful careers as business entrepreneurs, with multi-award-winning businesses in the United States, Australia, and New Zealand.

Now based in the U.S. and focused exclusively on personal transformation, Sandra and Daniel are the originators of a groundbreaking body of work, introduced in The CODEBREAKER PLATINUM Series. Presented with passion, intensity, grace, and wisdom, the Series is designed to empower individuals to build their own life of happiness, success, and fun — putting passion back into relationships, fulfillment and joy back into work, and restoring and enhancing health, vitality, and well-being.

Born in Australia, Sandra has always been an intuitive who spoke to Divine beings from the age of three when she told her mother she was here to work for God. Despite 36 death-defying surgeries, financial ruin, and divorce, Sandra's determination to succeed and to find the answers to the eternal questions of life, death, and love led her to become a self-made millionaire by the age of 29. She has diligently worked with some of the greatest spiritual teachers and success coaches throughout the world, and she is now a highly sought-after keynote speaker and workshop leader in personal transformation and enlightenment.

Born in America, Daniel has always dreamed of setting people free. To do that, he realized he first had to set himself free. Daniel had a 25-year career as owner and CEO in large-scale property development, with high-profile roles in civic, charitable, and industry leadership positions. His training encompassed a wide variety of spiritual traditions and deep experience in the human potential movement, as well as advanced business and management education and training.

When he met an Australian woman at one of her seminars in New Zealand, Daniel knew Sandra would rearrange his life forever. He proposed to her on their first date, and the next time they met, they agreed to be married. Sixteen years later, they still consider themselves newlyweds.

In their first project together, they created a private retreat in New Zealand to host spiritual intensives, which in its first year following completion won Condé Nast Traveler's highest rating in its Gold List of the world's Top 100 Hotels. It went on to be crowned The World's Best Luxury Coastal Hotel by the World Luxury Hotel Awards in 2010. In 2012, Eagles Nest received the World Travel Awards title of The World's Best Luxury Villa Boutique Resort.

Sandra and Daniel work with highly successful people who are committed to reaching the next level in their business and private lives — to be the best versions of themselves. Their clients are determined to successfully lean in to their lives — aware, mindful, and present. As Jack Canfield said, "They have an amazing ability to shift energy and remove blocks on very deep levels. They are the real deal."

From Sandra and Daniel:

Your thoughts are always the key variable in every situation. Training your mind to think thoughts that serve you is your highest priority. Becoming the best version of you is the most rewarding undertaking of all. It is an open-ended process in which we are continually reminded that the means and the ends must always be in harmony and integrity.

We have dedicated our lives to sharing our journey into enlightenment and wholeness. We invite you to share yours with us, and to move into higher and higher states of Integrated Wholeness together — to truly become the best versions of ourselves.

On our journey, we have invested many decades in study, research, and development. We have traveled the planet to sit with many leading spiritual teachers and energy masters. We have developed a turbocharged process for rapid change, which results in massive shifts within minutes as we neutralize blocks. We constantly witness people set free from the debilitating residue of trauma that years of therapy and counseling have been unable to shift. Using the higher awareness produced by The Ultimate Mind Shift™ process, we tap into what scientists call the human mind field to identify the underlying causes of any issue; then we use precise frequencies to neutralize them and delete their effects.

Like most people, we have had massive challenges throughout our lives. Using the work we teach, we not only survived, but thrived. For more than 40 years we have successfully worked with thousands of people around the world, and we have been gratified to achieve amazing results. We invite you to use us, and these books, as loving guides, mentors, trainers and coaches to support you on your journey.

You now have unprecedented opportunity and resources to make a quantum leap in your experience of life, and in the evolution of your soul. The decision is in your hands. Empower yourself to transform your life and to change your state to feel better — faster than you believe possible. Regardless of what you have or have not said or done, forgive yourself. Love yourself as we love you — fully, completely, and unconditionally. Embrace your calling and master the exhilarating role of being your own best friend — your own guru.

If you would like to know more about Sandra and Daniel, please visit **www.TheBiskinds.com**.

APPRECIATION

Throughout our lives, we have been blessed to have an enormous number of people make profound contributions to who we have become — and are still becoming. *AWARENESS: How Life Really Works* is the third of eight books in The CODEBREAKER PLATINUM Series. These books are a distillation of over 40 years of spiritual practice and study, powerful personal transformational experience, and our ongoing journey into becoming the best versions of ourselves.

With incredible gratitude to all the business and success mentors, coaches, transformational teachers, and spiritual and mystical masters who have touched our lives with your books, your workshops, and more importantly your presence, we say a truly heartfelt thank you. Thank you for your dedication in being the change we all seek, and for sharing who you are with the world.

A special thank you to Jack Canfield for taking the time to read *CODEBREAKER* and give us his feedback on a very rough first draft. He told us a book is not ready for publication until it has been rewritten at least six times, and encouraged us to get feedback from a minimum of 10 beta readers. Well, thanks to Jack, *CODEBREAKER: Discover The Password To Unlock The Best Version of You* was sent to over 30 people whose feedback was instrumental in helping us rewrite it — far more than six times. We decided to present each chapter as a book in its own right, and feedback confirmed the importance of releasing the books in the order they appear in the Master Password.

To everyone who has already read and re-read the

CODEBREAKER PLATINUM books, we cannot thank you enough for your support, wisdom, and thoughtfulness in making these books better in every way. To all the beta readers, editors, and developmental editors who shared their ideas on how to simplify and make a deep subject easier to comprehend, we are eternally grateful.

Writing these books has been a roller coaster ride of both excitement and overwhelming appreciation to so many people. Infinite gratitude goes to Bill Bryant and Sandy Beamer, who have devoted months to helping us in the rewriting process. Daily, they asked us to give better explanations of concepts that were new to them, or that they thought needed clarification or simplification. They wanted more examples, and more stories, to make the teaching more memorable.

Their lives have changed because of their total immersion into the information in each book. Can you imagine what a Godsend they were to us? After 40-plus years of committed spiritual transformation, practice, and study, with the one transcendent desire to live an enlightened life, they helped us break down deep concepts that were normal and natural to us into bite-size chunks, to make everything easier to digest and to use in *your* everyday life.

Deepest thanks and endless love to all our students, and our coaching and consulting clients, whose dedication and courage to move beyond limiting blocks keep us motivated to find better, faster, and more effective processes. You inspire us with your dedication, and honor us with your trust.

Our heartfelt thanks goes to our editor Rosina Wilson and our formatter Ramajon Cogan and also to the amazing Mary Giuseffi and Heidi Gress, who interpreted our cover ideas perfectly and helped us produce ILLUMINATION, the book cover designs for the series.

Finally, we want to thank all our family, and our friends who have become family, for your continued support and love. Without love, the world would be a cold and unfriendly place, instead of the warm, uplifting, and inspiring place we are so grateful to live in.

BECOME THE BEST VERSION OF YOU

Empowered Enlightened Inspired

THANK YOU! We hope you enjoyed the third book in The CODEBREAKER PLATINUM Series, and that you are now equipped with more tools to help you achieve freedom from unconscious programs and limiting beliefs; and to have the successful life and loving relationships you deserve.

You can rate this book, Tweet about it, and talk about it on Facebook. Please take a moment to do that. We'd be grateful, and it will help others who want to have a happier, more meaningful, and more fulfilled life.

We would also appreciate it if you could leave a short review of the book on Amazon via the link below. It will help us improve this and future books, and to help others like yourself decide if the books in this series are right for them.

Leave a review on Amazon. http://amzn.to/1h8vd0T

Also check out:

PEACE: *Power Up Your Life*

http://www.TheBiskinds.com/Peace

LOVE: *Ignite The Secret To Your Success*

http://www.TheBiskinds.com/Love

Post to FACEBOOK:

https://www.facebook.com/TheBiskinds

Tweet about this book: TWITTER:

https://twitter.com/TheBiskinds

https://twitter.com/DivineMindCode

PEACE

Fully connected to the light of my True Self,
Peace is my natural state.

PLATINUM

LOVE

Unconditional love is my essence.
My purpose is to grow, evolve and have
fun expressing the love that I am.

PLATINUM

AWARENESS

With awareness I intuitively see beyond ego mind stories
and understand the big picture.

PLATINUM

TRUST

I trust my True Self can discern the truth in any situation
which frees me from fear.

PLATINUM

INTEGRITY

My Integrity never compromises the means for an end so I am always whole and trustworthy.

PLATINUM

NEUTRALITY

Being neutral empowers me to realize
freedom and wholeness and to
have the life of my dreams.

PLATINUM

UNITY

Integrating unity and oneness makes it
natural for me to love and forgive
everyone and everything.

PLATINUM

MINDFULNESS

Mindfulness alerts me whenever I need to
correct negative thoughts, feelings,
and emotions to get neutral to be happy.

PLATINUM

PLATINUM

Made in the USA
Charleston, SC
12 October 2015